Management for Professionals

More information about this series at http://www.springer.com/series/10101

Carlos Cordon • Pau Garcia-Milà
Teresa Ferreiro Vilarino • Pablo Caballero

Strategy is Digital

How Companies Can Use Big Data in the Value Chain

Springer

7139

MT

Carlos Cordon
IMD
Lausanne, Switzerland

Teresa Ferreiro Vilarino
Barcelona, Spain

Pau Garcia-Milà
Valldoreix
Spain

Pablo Caballero
Accenture
Sant Cugat del Vallès
Spain

ISSN 2192-8096   ISSN 2192-810X   (electronic)
Management for Professionals
ISBN 978-3-319-80971-7   ISBN 978-3-319-31132-6   (eBook)
DOI 10.1007/978-3-319-31132-6

Printed on acid-free paper

This Springer imprint is published by Springer Nature
The registered company is Springer International Publishing AG Switzerland

2|8|19

Acknowledgements

The ideas of this book were developed with the help of Polina Bochukova and Jan Jelle van der Meer. They are the authors of Chap. 3, and they provided many insights for the other chapters.

Contents

Introduction

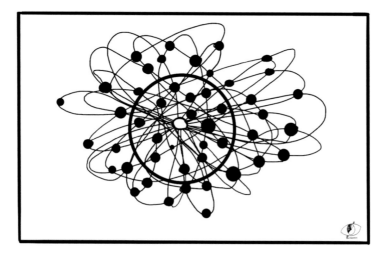

Big data is transforming everything. Consumers evolve and become much more proactive in their shopping journey. They check many websites and compare prices before they buy. In addition, technology is allowing us to extract knowledge from data that we could not utilize up until know. Furthermore, the Internet of Things, which refers to the data generated by physical devices connected to the web, is generating a huge amount of information that did not exist before. Companies need to adapt to the new reality to be able to compete. Big data is crucial not only for Internet-based businesses but also for traditional companies. Throughout this book, we explain how conventional businesses can seize the opportunities created by big data and embrace their own big data journey.

© Springer International Publishing Switzerland 2016
C. Cordon et al., *Strategy is Digital*, Management for Professionals,
DOI 10.1007/978-3-319-31132-6_1

1.1   Big Data Is Transforming Everything

Customers are evolving. In 2014 several reports indicated that more than 25 % of all Internet connections were made using mobile devices. This means that soon (if it is not already the case), more than half the visits to companies' websites will be via mobile phones. In fact, an Ofcom report published on August 6, 2015 stated that in the UK, "smartphones have overtaken laptops as the most popular device for getting online," as shown in Fig. 1.1 (Ofcom 2015).

This aspect of the big data revolution is just one of many affecting companies today. How does your company's website look on a mobile phone? Google penalizes websites that are not well adapted to mobiles by eliminating them from search results. But even if it is well adapted and provides a version easily readable on mobile phones and other devices, that will still not be enough to keep customers engaged.

Today's consumers are a lot more proactive in their shopping journeys. They consult companies' websites for information about products and where to buy them, they compare prices and consult forums for product reviews, and they do all this before even entering a store. In the shop they might use their devices to look up additional information, and if they cannot find what they are looking for, they may give up and go elsewhere.

Thus, a responsive website that adapts fonts, photographs and the visual layout automatically to the mobile screen will not in itself be sufficient to retain a customer's attention; sales will not grow and time-per-session using mobile phones will fall disastrously compared to time-per-session using personal computers.

The good news is that big data can fix this. A lot of information can be gleaned from users when they access a website. Analyzing this information will reveal the

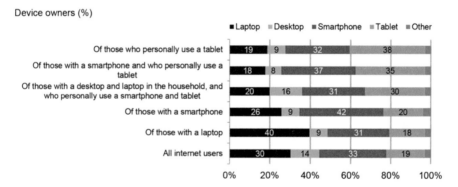

Base: Devices used by those who use the internet at home or elsewhere: Tablet (1528), smartphone & tablet (1276), desktop & laptop & smartphone & tablet (389), smartphone (2277), laptop (2214), all internet users (3095 UK).

QE11 (QE40): Which is the most important device you use to connect to the internet, at home or elsewhere? "Other" includes: "netbook," "games console," "other device," "none" and "don't know."

Fig. 1.1 Most important device for connecting to the Internet in the UK in Q1, 2015. *Source*: Ofcom Technology Tracker, Q1 2015

type of user and, for example, whether they are potential customers, investors, suppliers or just your mother looking for your office phone number.

How can all this be known? Let's take a look at what information can be collected from website visitors. It is possible to know what browser they are using and the operating system and screen resolution of their device. The IP address gives an idea about their geographical location. This information can be used to offer different products or information based on estimated purchasing power and statistics on the spending patterns of similar users.

There is one more thing that is important to understand about how users employ mobile phones when surfing the Internet. Mobile browsing brings with it constant interruptions, which can lead to poor concentration. Imagine you go to the office and a person you want to talk to is looking carefully at a website on their desktop computer. You stick your head between them and the screen and start yelling: "Stop reading right now because I want to talk to you." Does this seem odd? Well, that is exactly what happens when someone is deciding whether to buy a product from a website they accessed on their mobile phone and an incoming call interrupts them. The website suddenly disappears and the phone starts ringing, effectively telling the user to stop reading and answer the call.

This is a reality that consumers experience daily. To survive in this environment, companies need to prepare and adapt to what the market is demanding or risk losing sales, clients and precious leads.

The implications of big data go much deeper than changing consumer habits, however. Companies are evolving too. Some companies have reinvented their business model to survive. They have transformed who they are, what they do and why they do it. Obviously, not all businesses will see their ecosystems equally affected or need to reinvent themselves. But they will all have to understand where they stand and the extent of the big data impact around them in order to decide what direction to take and act accordingly.

1.2 This Book Is About Big Data and Business

Many of these changes have taken companies by surprise. Something that was seen as only affecting internet-based businesses like Google, Amazon, Facebook and Apple is now spreading and affecting all companies, including those created long before Google or Facebook were founded.

We started our research on big data and its impact on businesses because several top executives asked us to do so. Those executives could see that big data presented a huge opportunity. In fact, the results of several CEO surveys have highlighted big data as the top hot topic in the last years. Surprisingly, though, while CEOs can foresee the huge impact, many of their management teams and direct reports are simply choosing to ignore it.

Our objective with this book is to present our findings on how traditional companies—from toy manufacturers through logistics providers to pharmacy retailers and chemical companies—are seizing the opportunities created by big data. We also explain how these companies are navigating the big data journey and how other organizations can learn from them.

1.3   What Is Big Data?

Imagine if your mobile phone were to record every single place you had been, every second of the day, over several years. This would amount to a substantial amount of information. That is big data—a colossal volume of knowledge collected by all kinds of devices.

Wikipedia, probably the most-used knowledge resource, defines it thus: "Big data is a broad term for data sets so large or complex that traditional data processing applications are inadequate" (Wikipedia n.d.). Figure 1.2 illustrates well what most people understand by big data.

Gartner, the company that introduced the term big data, defined it as "high-volume, -velocity and -variety information assets that demand cost-effective,

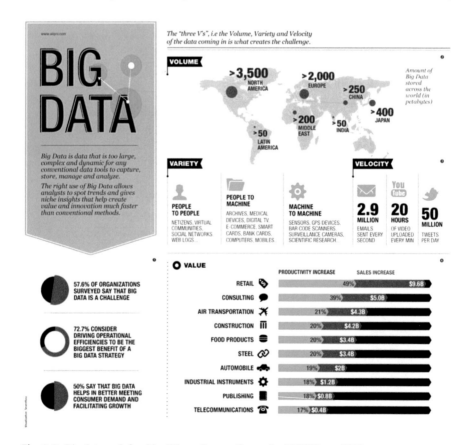

Fig. 1.2 Big data as defined by Wipro. *Source*: Survey by EIU/Wipro, 2013

innovative forms of information processing for enhanced insight and decision making" (Gartner n.d.). This definition, with its three Vs, quickly became the standard definition. Later on, the fourth and fifth Vs, veracity and value—which many experts claim are the most relevant—were added. Because if the data is incorrect or useless, what would be the point in collecting it? The patterns revealed by analyzing big data, and a company's ability to take decisions based on those insights, are what give big data its value.

Some experts also talk about "dark data," which refers to information that cannot be exploited or used because there are no tools able to do so. However, as technology evolves, this "dark data" is being turned into information that can be used. Take the example of videos on YouTube. Until recently nobody would have dreamt of using computers to analyze their content. Today, several companies have computers "watching" every single TV channel and identifying how many seconds each brand is shown in adverts and movies. That would have been unthinkable just a few years ago.

The volume of data is now growing more dramatically than ever with the popularity of smartphones, wearable devices and the Internet of Things (IoT), which refers to the data generated by physical devices that are connected to and accessed through the web. The adoption of smartphones by the general public took off in 2009. Their use constantly generates all kinds of data. This, combined with the expansion of social media and the ease of posting and sharing content on the web directly from a smartphone, has further accelerated the growth of big data.

In 2010 the IoT gained momentum and within a year it was producing roughly as much data as all personal devices. Where did the IoT come from? Why then? According to Cisco, the IoT was born around 2008 or 2009, the inflexion point at which the number of gadgets connected to the network exceeded the number of people on earth (Evans 2011). While in 2010 there were 500 million devices connected, or 1.84 connected devices per person, predictions indicate that by 2020 there will be 50 billion devices connected, or 6.58 per person.

Thus, big data is just a huge amount of data and we have now reached the tipping point at which it can be used meaningfully and exploited to change the way we do business.

1.4   Discovering Big Data in Existing Businesses

When we began our research on how big data was changing existing businesses we expected a few surprises. We did not anticipate so many and such vast changes. We sought out companies with interesting initiatives but found only a few: LEGO, the toy company; Mediq, a Dutch healthcare company; some pharmaceutical companies; a few logistics companies; some insurance companies; a US grocery and pharmacy retailer; and even a company that uses space rockets to conduct scientific research. We also found that in 2014 a Hong Kong venture capital fund appointed a computer program as one of its board members, to make investment recommendations just like any other member (Wile 2014). It was the first time a robot had held such a highly qualified position. Until then, robots had only been assigned low-level tasks. We further discovered that a lot of companies should have been implementing big data initiatives but were just waiting for the tsunami to catch them.

The biggest surprise was among the pharmaceutical companies. In Chap. 3 we explain how a law aimed at eliminating the trade of counterfeit drugs is forcing pharmaceutical companies to join an initiative that is essentially a big data journey. It could be a great opportunity for these organizations to dramatically improve the way they do business, but the reality is that most are just trying to comply with new regulations and are not planning to use this as an opportunity to create more value.

One exception is Mediq, which used the opportunity to redefine its business as "taking care of patients" instead of just "moving boxes," and making money from minimizing the number of hospitalizations resulting from inappropriate drug use. It is quite astonishing that it has been able to use big data to contribute to improving the health of its clients while at the same time increasing its revenue.

The biggest surprise, though, was discovering that in many sports, big data is considered essential to win. For example, the most successful swimming coach in terms of the number of Olympic gold medals won by his coachees claims that the difference between qualifying and winning a gold medal is big data. It is amazing to think that winning a global swimming competition could depend on statistics.

1.5   How This Book Is Organized

This book compiles all that we have learned over 2 years of research. Our objective was to find successful stories of early adopters to gain a glimpse of the future. The book aims to lead you through the big data journey and help your company embrace the change. It is about the stories, the tools and the frameworks that you will need on the way.

In Chap. 2 we use the example of LEGO to describe how companies' strategies and business models are changing as a result of big data. We provide several tools and frameworks to help you to redefine your strategy and embed big data in it.

Chapter 3 looks into how legal requirements to trace medical drugs at every stage—from manufacture to delivery to patients—have pushed pharmaceutical companies to initiate their big data journeys. Many of them are just fulfilling their obligations without taking advantage of big data capabilities. We look in detail at Mediq, which, unlike most, transformed itself to integrate big data into its business, increasing its profitability to twice that of its peers. These changes are impacting the whole value chain.

In Chap. 4 we explain a new concept that describes a different kind of value chain made possible by big data and that is a logical response to omnichannel consumerism: the **omnichain**. Big data makes it possible to design much more complex value chains that are managed intelligently and autonomously and that interact with all the other players in the value chain, exchanging places and roles when convenient. The chapter brims with examples the show how omnichains are going to revolutionize global value chains.

Chapter 5 explores the world of logistics and transportation. The massive rise in the volume of e-commerce is creating a huge challenge as well as many opportunities in the way logistics are managed to deliver quickly while reducing costs. On the one hand, traditional players like Yamato Logistics have to rely on big data to survive. On the other hand, new players from different industries are leveraging their big data know-how to enter an industry that, up until now, was only accessible to a few. The chapter describes the challenges and opportunities in this section of the value chain.

Chapter 6 helps you take the next steps in your own big data journey using a new framework to transform your company and adapt it to the big data era. It combines four existing methodologies that differ greatly from traditional ones. Five-year business plans are a thing of the past. Big data implies constantly innovating, testing, exchanging information and learning in an endless cycle. We explain how that works. Furthermore, traditional industry analyses are ill equipped for navigating blurry industry boundaries where everybody competes with everybody, so we provide a proven framework to help manage this.

In Chap. 7 we conclude by summarizing the key learnings and implications of big data for businesses.

1.6   How to Use This Book

The book can be used in many ways. You can read it from beginning to end. Or, if you are short of time, you could just read the parts most relevant to your needs. Table 1.1 summarizes what to read depending on the time at your disposal and your particular interests.

Every chapter is intended to be self-contained and can be read independently of the others. This inevitably means that you will find some repetition should you read the entire book in one go. We ask for your forgiveness if that is the case.

Whether you read the whole book or just parts of it, we hope you find it useful as you embark on your own big data journey.

Finally, we are all learning continuously, and in this era of collaboration, we encourage you to share your journey with other organizations in your ecosystem.

Table 1.1 How to read this book

Time at your disposal/Area of interest	Suggested reading
No time	Chapters 1 and 7
Very little time	Chapters 1, 2, 6 and 7
Interested in the healthcare industry?	Chapter 3
Interested in supply chain evolutions?	Chapter 4
Interested in logistics and e-commerce?	Chapter 5

References

Evans, Dave. The Internet of Things. How the Next Evolution of the Internet Is Changing Everything. Cisco IBSG, April 2011. http://www.cisco.com/web/about/ac79/docs/innov/IoT_IBSG_0411FINAL.pdf. Accessed August 13, 2015.

Gartner IT Glossary. http://www.gartner.com/it-glossary/big-data. Accessed August 13, 2015.

Ofcom. 2015. The communications market 2015. The Market in Context. http://stakeholders.ofcom.org.uk/binaries/research/cmr/cmr15/UK_1.pdf. Accessed August 13, 2015.

Wikipedia. N.d. Big Data. https://en.wikipedia.org/wiki/Big_data. Accessed August 13, 2015.

Wile, Rob. 2014. A venture capital firm just named an algorithm to its board of directors—Here's what it actually does. Business Insider. May 13. http://www.businessinsider.com/vital-named-to-board-2014-5. Accessed August 13, 2015.

From Digital Strategy to Strategy Is Digital

2

2.1 Evolution of Digital in the Enterprise

The tsunami-like smartphone revolution has fundamentally reshaped consumer behavior. It has caught retailers by surprise by bringing changes that were unforeseeable just a few years ago. This in turn is affecting value chains, which are becoming much more agile. And some organizations are adapting their products to incorporate digital features into traditionally physical experiences. All of these shifts are a result of big data.

2.1.1 The Omnichannel

Today's consumers use multiple channels and sources to decide which products they want and where to buy them. For example, instead of spending their Saturday

© Springer International Publishing Switzerland 2016
C. Cordon et al., *Strategy is Digital*, Management for Professionals,
DOI 10.1007/978-3-319-31132-6_2

in shops looking to see what is available and comparing prices, they might start by checking a product's website, consulting forums or Facebook for consumer reviews. If they decide to buy it, they search on Internet for the best price and place to buy it, either online or onsite. This by no means suggests that physical shops are no longer important. Two-thirds of consumers who buy online visit stores beforehand or afterward (ATKearney 2014). From the customer viewpoint, the apps, the physical store and the website are all part of the same purchasing experience. Recent research revealed that 42 % of shoppers search for information on the Internet while in the store, and 71 % of those who do so say that their device has become more important to their in-store experience (Think with Google 2014).

This is equally valid for car buyers. Research reveals that consumers go through five stages on the path to purchasing a vehicle, and digital plays an important role at each stage. Most of the journey—filtering and assessing options—is completed online. Usually they only visit the dealership at the end (Microsoft 2012).

The result of adapting the distribution channel to these new behaviors is the omnichannel. Companies are developing new strategies to engage with their consumers, offering them a consistent, seamless experience across all channels. Retailers, for example, can use their online presence—website, apps, mobile ads and search results—to assist customers in the store and improve their experience.

These fundamental changes were made possible as a result of big data and, more specifically, the ability of modern technology to take advantage of it.

2.1.2   After the Omnichannel, the Omnichain

Just as marketing and sales are experiencing major evolutions as a result of the big data revolution, so are value chains being radically transformed as they adapt to this new situation. Value chains used to be designed around physical constraints that assumed limited access to information about products and their location. They had to be planned in a consolidated way, with large-scale production based on huge orders because of limited computer power and access to data. Thus companies traditionally made large batches of a product, say a shirt with red buttons, and then tried to sell these on. Now they increasingly produce on demand and build value chains based on the specific needs of customers as the big data revolution is transforming value chains into omnichains capable of designing, producing, planning and delivering products and services for small orders.

An omnichain is an ecosystem in which companies interact to complement each other's capabilities in view of delivering a product or service to the customer. Any player within the ecosystem can change and assume new positions fast. For example, it might be that for one product, company A does the dyeing and company B the manufacturing and assembly, while for another product company A does the dyeing and manufacturing and company B assembles the final item (see Fig. 2.1).

Omnichain activities are allocated within the ecosystem dynamically. The actor orchestrating the value chain picks the best combination of suppliers of goods and/or service in each case. Founded over a century ago, Hong-Kong-based

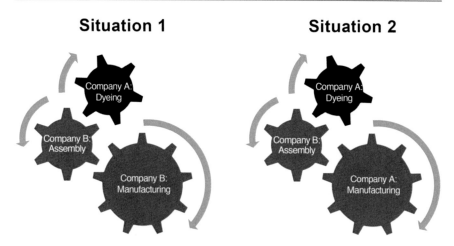

Fig. 2.1 Dynamic value chain

multinational Li & Fung has been doing this for decades. Its customers, which include companies like Walmart, come to it to buy products with a value chain spread across Asia. Li & Fung creates a customized supply chain for each product by selecting, managing and coordinating a network of suppliers that will make it according to the customer's specific requirements. So for example, if company A wants shirts with red buttons, Li & Fung will select the fabric supplier, the red button supplier, the manufacturer, the distributor and so forth. If at some point the customer requests the same shirt but with blue buttons, Li & Fung will adapt the chain to accommodate this.

Omnichains are modular, which means that parts can be handled independently, making it easy to reconfigure the chain swiftly. A company can create its own omnichain by selecting the members of its ecosystem and assigning tasks in the best way to achieve the desired revenue, risk profile or time-to-market. Digitalization and big data are making this possible on a much greater scale. What's more, as the Mediq example illustrates, more sophisticated value propositions combining products and services are being developed.

> *Mediq is a Dutch healthcare company (see Chap. 3) that used to simply buy products from manufacturers and distribute them to pharmacies or directly to people at home. Its main activity was "moving boxes" from one place to another. Now, using big data, Mediq has transformed its value chain to "taking care of the patient." It collects data from its customers and uses it to help improve patients' health by advising them about their treatments (for example when to take their medicine) and informing doctors about complementary treatments, such as a stomach protection to take with anti-*

(continued)

inflammatories for example. Its new business model has brought down the number of patients needing hospitalization as a result of inadequate use of their medication, which in turn has reduced the costs of medical insurance companies. Mediq was able to demonstrate and quantify such savings and agreed with insurance companies to share those benefits 50:50. Mediq is thus playing a much more encompassing role in the value chain.

2.1.3 Digital Fusion in the Consumer Experience

One thing triggering these transformations is the evolution of the consumer profile. Many consumers, especially younger ones, now combine digital and physical worlds in the same experience (playing games, shopping). For them, the virtual and physical worlds are naturally integrated as part of the same reality.

The toy industry has adapted to this evolution. In order to fit into this new landscape and keep their young consumers engaged, toy companies have developed new lines of products. LEGO created LEGO Fusion, a set of games that merge physical and digital realities. Users first download a LEGO app to their smartphone or tablet and purchase the physical LEGO fusion kit. Users then build a physical object using their kit. They capture this design using their smartphone or tablet and make it come to life using their smart device to accomplish game missions. At any time the user can go back and adapt or rebuild the physical object to continuously shape their experience according to their own imagination (see Fig. 2.2).

The implications of digital fusion are far from trivial. A time will likely come when users will no longer be interested in the physical experience alone because it will be incomplete. To survive, some companies will have to review their mission and strategy and adapt to the new reality.

2.1.4 Adapting to Digital Fusion: The LEGO Experience

2.1.4.1 Big Data to Interact with Consumers

When it comes to relationships with end users, most companies in the toy industry have built a powerful social media presence. Their goal is to offer users a consistent experience across all channels, a challenge in itself mainly for two reasons. First, social media are dynamic and quickly become outmoded—some of the most successful networks 5 years ago are now just a distant memory. Second, these companies have so many products that creating a specific digital experience for each product results in a fragmented overall experience for the user, something to be avoided because fragmentation also often implies that the information collected by each unit is not shared with the rest of the company.

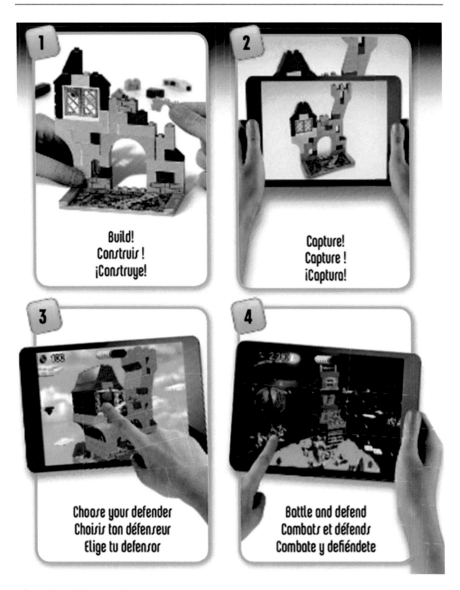

Fig. 2.2 LEGO (n.d.) fusion

To avoid fragmentation and ensure data could be shared, LEGO designed its ecosystem to combine all its digital consumer platforms into a single experience for users. It was conceived to be beneficial both for the consumer and the company. Consumers would benefit from a richer experience because they could connect all the dots of their LEGO world. The company would benefit from the centralized information about each user and an improved database that made it easier to handle the consumer data. It was expected that as a result, LEGO's consumers would be happier, meaning they would be closer and more loyal to the brand.

2.1.4.2 Big Data for More Effective Marketing

Big data provides detailed information that allows companies to understand consumers and their behaviors much better and thus micro-segment and target them more effectively. Up until recently, companies knew more or less who their clients were, where to find them and how to reach them, but the error margin was high as they relied on information collected from a sample of volunteers who agreed to have a device installed at home to report what was being watched on television. Companies usually ended up extending their target groups to make sure they reached their real audience. Not only were the costs high but also the TV commercials were not necessarily watched by their target audience. Cable and digital media made it possible to know who was watching what and when, so the whole audience—not just a sample—could be tracked all of the time. Companies could thus devise accurate and micro-segmented campaigns aimed at specific groups of consumers, which was a great deal more effective and considerably cheaper. This micromarketing of products or services to a small segment of the market can now, thanks to big data, be used on a large scale.

LEGO had agreements with TV cable providers, which could tell it when its potential buyers (say mothers in their 30s with one or two children) were in front of their TV. This allowed the company to address these particular consumers at specific times of the day at a much lower cost.

2.1.4.3 Big Data to Ensure a Common Language

Not everything about big data is beneficial. Old problems considered resolved some time ago have resurfaced. In the beginning, computers occupied around 70 % of an entire room. In the 1980s that same room was used as a "data warehouse" where technical guys played and experimented with data. The huge platforms, usually based on IBM mainframes, made it possible for companies to start collecting vast amounts of information. But the data meant different things depending on who used it. In a given multinational, one country might include the impact of its discounts in its net sales profits when uploading its sales data; another country might use a different formula and exclude discounts from its net sales data. To be able to compare the information (in this case sales) from different countries, companies had to ensure that everyone used the same parameters. Software companies offered programs to cleanse and integrate all the data to eliminate invalid information and ensure better quality final data.

Nestlé, for example, made a huge effort to standardize the information it used throughout the organization. Its massive GLOBE Program helped everyone agree on a common language to refer to the internal functioning (Killing 2003). By the time its Globe project had been rolled out globally, all business units and countries were using the same definitions for the data they stored: net or gross sales meant the same thing in every country and in every business unit. This achievement was only possible because all of its internal information was stored on the same database (SAP). Today, Nestlé again faces the challenge of obtaining reliable and integrated information because, according to Everett (2012), "Companies store huge amounts of structured and unstructured information from various sources and formats, and this data needs to be governed, cleansed and integrated so that it can be used to build predictive models and make decisions." Even after this has been completed, there will still be some invalid data among the validated information, but Nestlé will have to learn to live with that.

LEGO understood the importance of high-quality big data for making strategic decisions. But its database was fed with huge amounts of information that did not follow common criteria, so the information that was extracted was unreliable. It was imperative to develop a new solution with a common definition of data throughout the company, and to cleanse the data to ensure consistency and offer a "single version of the truth"[1] instead of many:

In 2012 LEGO took on the great challenge of what it called the Business Intelligence Concept Foundation (BICF), whose main objective was to achieve standardization data-wise. Until then data was stored centrally but handled locally by the various business units, which created reports following guidelines provided by their direct leader rather than by corporate standards. These were often very time-consuming and useless reports that served the purpose of just one person. In addition, users accessing the system could pull up a report from the data they selected based on their own interpretation, which resulted in a loss of rigor and trustworthiness. It was necessary to put the existing data in order and give them more value by creating standard reports available to all business units (Cordón and Ferreiro 2015).

---

[1] Term used by Mark Rittman to define the need for a company to have integrated and reliable data that would provide a "single version of the truth" (Rittman 2006).

2.1.4.4 Big Data to Reshape the Business Model

The use of big data may impact business models on two levels. First, it can help organizations manage their existing business models. Up until now those that had several business models had to manage them all in the same way. Big data eliminates this constraint because it opens up new ways of operating. Second, big data can generate new business models. If LEGO started making money from selling its apps, this would generate a new business model that would need to be managed differently.

LEGO launched its HORIZON Project to process company information throughout the value chain.

HORIZON was born out of a desire to match LEGO's IT with the way it operated as a company. When HORIZON started, a lot of work had already been done to establish an integrated value chain based on a physical infrastructure supporting it. Also the global operating principles had been defined.

The full execution of this strategic direction was, however, limited by the IT set-up designed and implemented many years previously. But the new business landscape was much more diverse. There was a fast-changing retail landscape that included on the one hand the addition of new markets, and on the other the digitalization of the play experience. This evolution transformed the whole value chain but the IT system had not yet adapted to it. LEGO ran on SAP, an IT-integrated model that brought together all the company information in a big database. Its main constraint was that the present SAP set-up was designed for a different business reality. To compensate for this discordance LEGO needed to rely on manual interventions, many Excel sheets and customization to the system. ... The HORIZON project tried to resolve the situation. It also acknowledged the need for flexibility to improve responsiveness (Cordón and Ferreiro 2015).

2.1.5   How Big Data Will Impact Traditional Businesses

We saw at the beginning of this chapter how consumers are integrating digital into their shopping journey, which has become more complex as a result of the many different channels that people are using on their purchasing path. Businesses need to adapt to this shift toward the use of multiple channels in the purchasing process, referred to as the omnichannel.

The omnichannel has brought as a consequence the development of the omnichain—still fairly recent and probably not applicable to all industries. Unlike the traditional static value chain, the omnichain is dynamic in that it consists of independent modules that can be re-configured and re-connected in real time depending on the company's needs.

The omnichain is starting to become a reality in a world in which many new consumers combine digital and physical worlds as part of a single product or

Fig. 2.3 Business models

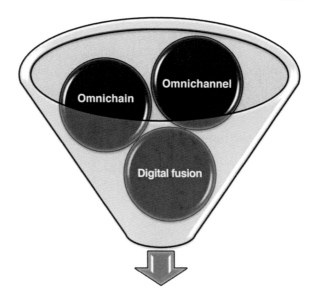

Business models

service experience: the digital fusion. Many companies will need to adapt to this to keep customers engaged. For that they will need to reshape their business models and probably create new ones (Fig. 2.3).

In our opinion, all companies should care about how the big data revolution will affect their business. Its impact could be reflected at different levels. It may only affect the company's marketing aspects or it may require a rethink of the entire value chain, including relationships with suppliers. Some companies may even find that they need to revolutionize their products, services and business models. Whatever the case may be, the big data journey has started, and sooner or later all organizations will need to react. Changes that are apparently small may have huge effects, as e-commerce has proven. In January 2014, *Business Insider* published an article (Peterson 2014), which it followed up by a documentary on WBIR.com a year later (Butera and Donila 2015), in which it warned that shopping malls across America were shutting down. It predicted that only one-third of all shopping malls were generating a profit at the time, 10 % of US malls would fail by 2022, and only half of those existing today would still be open by 2025. Why? There are many reasons. Changing American lifestyles is one of them. Teenagers are now the number one group shopping at malls. The groups that were important mall shoppers years ago (baby boomers, empty nesters and millennials) do not want to hang out with teenagers. The decline of the middle class due to economic crises is also a contributing factor, as is the development of e-commerce. Although the e-commerce sales market share is not enormous at 6.1 % of the total in 2014, decreasing to 5.5 % in 2018 (eMarketer 2014), it is enough to account for shopping-mall closures because it is destabilizing the retail ecosystem.

Another example—that is apparently small but could be highly disruptive—is the taxi industry and how it has been affected by Uber.

Uber, considered by Time as one of the best apps of the year in 2013 (Aamoth 2013), has been shut down in some countries because taxi drivers were losing too much business. The app connects drivers and passengers, who can enjoy a private ride for a lower rate than in a normal taxi. It seemed impossible that a traditional industry sector like this could be affected by a smartphone application, but it was. Uber's market penetration was not huge and was not expected to grow more than 10% of the total market share in the overall market in the future (Damodaran 2014), but this was enough to spur all taxi lobbies to fight to have Uber closed down because it was taking too much income from traditional taxi companies. In fact, small as it might seem, Uber was serious business. Valued at $40 billion in December 2014 (Bradshaw 2014), its market capitalizations exceeded those of Twitter, LinkedIn or transport companies such as American Airlines, Hertz and Avis. In the meantime, other industry sectors like warehousing or home delivery are starting to apply Uber's business model.

2.2 Designing a Digital Strategy

Our research for this book revealed that companies were reacting to big data in different ways. Some were basing their strategy on big data in that their new strategy had become digital. Others had implemented a master plan to integrate big data into their strategy. Yet others had not experienced a lot of impact to their ecosystem.

We believe that all companies will need to hypothesize to what extent their respective industry sector will be affected by the big data transformation and design an appropriate strategy. Depending on the outcome of the hypothesis, companies may opt for one of the following three strategies:

Digital Fit: Taking Advantage of Big Data Innovations In this scenario, the business of the company does not change dramatically with the implementation and use of big data. This could, for example, be the case of a B2B chemical company with a small number of customers and suppliers. It will probably apply big data to its internal functioning (sensors, machinery, etc.) but will not experience major changes in strategy. Big data will not change its essence but will help it improve in a number of areas such as customer service, operational savings or inventory handling.

Digital Masterplan: Implementing Big Data Companies in this category will implement a digital strategy into their corporate strategy but it will not become their core business. Fast-moving consumer goods companies such as soft-drink manufacturers will need to include a digital master plan in their overall strategy to deal with big data. They will receive information from consumers, be able to get to know them better and extract behavioral patterns, which might lead to a new selling or communication strategy; retailers will expect cost reductions from leveraging learnings from big data. Information gleaned from big data could prompt a company to change the way it distributes its products, as was the case 15 years ago when companies sold or shared point-of-sales information to manufacturers to obtain price reductions. Now retailers are providing big data information to manufacturers in exchange for part of the savings achieved as a result of using this information. Soft drinks manufacturers will therefore have to adapt their overall strategy and design a big data masterplan to support it.

Digital DNA: Becoming Digital These companies will mutate as implementing big data will fundamentally transform their business model. This will also require a change of strategy to one driven by the use of big data. Some organizations are already integrating big data into the core of their business. Insurance company Axa is using big data to consolidate a better picture of risk (Axa 2014). Its brokers have real-time access to information from a wide range of public sources, which they use to tailor their approach and insurance solution to each client. Axa has changed its insurance offerings, the criteria it uses to choose between them, and the way it collects information from its customers. The whole business has been transformed by big data. Car insurers also used big data to develop the "pay-as-you-drive" concept where the premium is calculated dynamically based on the driver's behavior, which is monitored while the person drives (National Association of Insurance Commissioners 2015).

Agreeing on the best strategy may not be straightforward. The toy industry is certainly experiencing a situation that could go in many directions. All industry players seem to agree that digital fusion is a fundamental change that is here to stay. But to what extent will this justify a complete shift in company strategy? A toy company may choose to become digital from its core and adapt all its toys and games to a digital ecosystem, or it may choose to just create a strong digital strategy, using big data to manage its relationship with customers and suppliers and for marketing for example, and leave the essence of the company (and its toys) intact.

2.2.1 The Evolution of Corporate Strategy

Having decided on the most appropriate strategy, the big question is, how to take the organization in the chosen direction? Over the years, companies have used a number of strategic models to design their corporate strategies. Each of these models has proved to be effective in some situations but less so in others. Below, we describe the key ones and how they have adapted to the changing circumstances over time.

2.2.1.1 The Industry Analysis

Until recently, companies still churned out 5-year business plans. An industry analysis was one of the key elements used to understand their current situation and plan from there. This involved analyzing the environment, the context and the competition to define how they should position themselves within their industry. In 1979 Michael Porter introduced his Five Forces to help companies develop their corporate strategy concept (Porter 1979). As he explained, five forces shaped all industries. By understanding how each force behaved in a given industry, companies could gain a good understanding of the battlefield, which helped them spot new opportunities and threats and gave them a basis on which to develop a competitive strategy.[2]

That was over 35 years ago and companies used the model for over 30 years. It was a valuable tool when industries were stable and well defined, when companies knew who their competitors were, and when firms could recognize the suppliers and consumers they were dealing with and more or less predict their behavior. Meanwhile, however, industry boundaries blurred and identifying new competitors became harder in a world where everybody can compete with everybody, as demonstrated by Nike.

> *In May 2006 sports footwear manufacturer Nike released the first version of its Nike iPod Sports Kit, an activity tracker that measured the distance covered, the pace and the calories burned by the user. Since then Nike has been adapting its app for all types of devices, including the Apple Watch. With this first move in 2006, Nike had expanded its boundaries to become a technological player competing with companies in different industries. Activity tracking devices like Fitbit and app developers like Samsung witnessed Nike taking a chunk of their market when it entered new spaces that stretched far beyond the sports-shoes manufacturing industry.*
>
> *Nike had already started its expansion into other industry sectors years before, with a strategy based on acquisitions, including of apparel companies. This meant that it was no longer just making sports shoes; it was also manufacturing a whole range of sportswear. In 2002, for example, it bought surfwear titan Hurley International (Earnest 2002).*

In this new environment, where players operated in and interconnected different industries, it was difficult and inaccurate to identify Porter's Five Forces. A change of perspective was needed.

---

[2] The five forces are: (1) Threats of new entrant competitors, (2) threats of new products, (3) bargaining power of the consumers, (4) bargaining power of the suppliers and (5) the number and activity of a company's rivals.

2.2.1.2 Defining the Company's Core Competencies

The next step was to switch from looking outside at the industry and planning moves based on the external environment to looking inward to understand and maximize the company's strengths. The time of the core competency analysis had arrived whereby organizations focused on what they did well—their core competencies—and outsourced the rest. Nokia is a good example of this period.

> Nokia was founded in 1865 as a paper mill. By 1912 it had expanded to include five lines of business: rubber, cable, forestry, electronics and power generation. In 1960 it entered the telecommunications industry. Later, it made the strategic decision to make telecommunications its core business, and between 1989 and 1996 it divested all of its basic industry and non-telecommunications businesses (Nokia n.d.). To maintain its position as the world leader in mobile phones, the company needed to focus on and invest in what it was good at and eliminate what was not core and could divert the company from its objectives. Nokia knew well that, at that time, its strength was in designing mobile phone architecture and usability so it invested all its resources in that and outsourced the components it was not so good at, such as the cameras and screens, to partner companies that were leaders in their particular field. It was a win-win situation: Nokia avoided wasting time and money re-inventing a good optical, and third parties that were good at making cameras entered new market niches by adapting their cameras to mobile phones.

Over time, Nokia lost its ability to adapt so well to its environment. We discuss later in this chapter how, in order to succeed, companies (especially in technology) need to know their environment and learn its rules, based mainly on collaboration. Interacting in this environment implies integrating other players' best practices rather than trying to do things based on core competencies alone like Nokia did (Cord 2014).

Once companies had defined the key competencies they wanted to focus on and which ones they could drop or outsource, the next step was to execute a strategy to maximize them.

2.2.1.3 Must-Win Battles

All the models we have seen so far[3] had common shortcomings. They provided executives with the tools they needed to design corporate strategies, but they did not explain how to put them into practice, and executives inevitably stumbled at that point. They needed to know where to start and how to prioritize.

---

[3] For more information about other models (e.g., Blue Ocean Strategies) see Appendix 1 to this chapter.

Malnight et al. (2006) book *Must-Win Battles* filled the void by offering companies tools to help them remain focused and execute their strategies. Their hands-on model proposed a way to first identify the key critical challenges that can cause a company to fail or succeed, and second, to create a short list of three to five "must-wins" that were indispensable to the company's success. Executives would need to learn to recognize which battles could be lost, avoided or handled by seeking consensus.

In 2001 Carlsberg and Orkla joined forces to become Carlsberg Breweries. In November 2002 the top management team met and agreed to focus on "must-win battles" to achieve their objectives. In May 2003, after noticing that their Q1 2003 results were below market expectations, they reviewed their must-win battles to focus on market performance and cost effectiveness. By August 2003 results were improving and within 2 years of the merge, the new company had become the fastest-growing beer brand in the world (Malnight 2007).

In 2012 Nike decided to sell some of its apparel brands to "focus on accelerating growth through Nike and complementary sports brands" (Nike 2012). This shift in the company's strategy resulted from the realization that it could not reach everywhere. It thus decided to focus on the battles it could win and drop those that were not crucial for the business.

2.2.2   The Business Model

Over time, many authors, including Thomas Malnight himself, have acknowledged that blurring traditional industry boundaries has prompted businesses to adopt a new concept: the ecosystem (Malnight et al. 2013).

An ecosystem weaves together various organizations such as suppliers, distributors, customers, competitors, government agencies and so on who collaborate and compete to deliver products or services. Each company affects and is affected by the others, and the relationship constantly evolves. So, in order to survive, each business needs to be flexible and adaptable, just like in a biological ecosystem.

The models we have seen so far either fail to take into consideration the ecosystem or, if they do, they just assume that you know the ecosystem your company is part of. But today's existing uncertainty implies that we do not necessarily know our battlefield. The Business Model Canvas proposed by Alexander Osterwalder and Yves Pigneur in their book *Business Model Generation* (2010) was initially a tool for new technological startups seeking investors. The IT industry is characterized by an extreme need for collaboration among various parties. Software, hardware and Internet companies always need to interact, partner, rely on and compete with others in order to survive. It is a dynamic business environment. Venture capitalists need to understand how a business will become profitable, but these startups were creating products and services that did not exist up until then, so it was not easy for them to give an answer and define a strategy using existing models. Besides, explaining their strategy required describing the ecosystem that they were part of and its rules. *Business Model Generation* allowed them to define their strategy and explain their business model in a nutshell.

> *Apple is one company that has mastered its ecosystem. Initially, the company developed physical products like the Mac and the iPhone. Then it created a few digital elements such as iTunes and the Apple Store to connect and enhance its digital products. Today, suppliers are continuously creating apps for Apple devices and selling these through the Apple Store, which benefits both parties. The music that is sold on iTunes to be played on an iPod or iPhone is a source of income for Apple, so it has effectively extended its ecosystem to benefit from far more sources of income than its own products.*

The ecosystem is characterized by strong relationships with other companies. One of the consequences of this new, more complex business environment is that it is no longer as straightforward as it once was to know where a company makes its money. The Profit Formula helps to clarify this by looking at the impact of several key indicators on the overall revenues.

These two concepts, the Business Model Canvas and the Profit Formula, have become so important that we have dedicated Chap. 6 of this book to them.

2.3   A New Framework for Developing Strategies

In order to adapt to these new times, companies need new tools to develop their strategies. We propose the "portfolio of options" because companies will find themselves having to address dilemmas that did not exist before and for which there is no right or wrong solution. Developing several potential scenarios is a good way for leaders to visualize the future of their organization and design different strategies in each case.

2.3.1   Developing a Portfolio of Options

The only way for companies to adapt their strategy to today's reality, which is characterized by rapid and unpredictable change across the globe, is by defining a portfolio of strategic initiatives based on multiple criteria and selecting from the resulting matrix the best options to implement at any given moment. For example, in Fig. 2.4, the two main criteria are (1) the **risk** that these initiatives will imply for

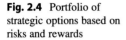

Fig. 2.4 Portfolio of strategic options based on risks and rewards

the company and (2) the value—or **reward**—that they will bring. Each organization will need to create its own matrix based on its key drivers.

A strategy will be required to guide the decision on the most appropriate option.

In 2007 Tetra Pak was conscious that the company had too many strategic initiatives—40 to 60—that overlapped and did not have a clear governance system. Country organizations were bombarded with initiatives from headquarters that they were realistically unable to implement, and that sometimes did not even have a clear business case. The company cut them to 25, and put in place a whole transformation process at a senior level, including the CEO, with a clear governance system: five different councils (strategy, transformation, product & technology, capability and corporate governance) reported to the executive team. Headed by the CEO, the strategy council had to sign off on a given direction and review each set of initiatives twice a year to ensure continued alignment with strategic objectives and the market reality.

Transformation was managed as a process (...). Before beginning a new initiative, it was verified that there was a clear link to the strategy, a business case and resources, and clear accountability. Senior managers were responsible for presenting the closure chart when the initiative was finished.

In 2011 Tetra Pak had the governance in place to successfully manage its portfolio of initiatives, cascading corporate projects down to regions, and prioritizing projects to ensure appropriate resourcing. (Büchel et al. 2011)

Normally your company will have a number of initiatives in each box. The key is to know how to combine them to ensure that the organization is ready for a new external global shift without being damaged. Company A might decide to invest 80 % of its current budget in low-low strategic initiatives and dedicate 20 % to creating a new product and expanding to the Asia market. Company B might decide to play it more risky by assigning 60 % of its budget to a low-low strategic approach, and investing the other 40 % in high-high initiatives to explore new markets and/or products. A good approach to the portfolio of options is to always place most financial assets on a controlled-risk strategy (low-low), and use blue-sky thinking to play with the other options, learning from the feedback on actions and reinvesting.

2.3.2   The Dilemma of Integration Versus Experimentation and Autonomy

During this process, companies may face the significant dilemma of having to choose between company integration (or centralization) versus autonomy (or decentralization).

Integrating the company's information and processes will allow it to synchronize not only its IT systems but also its company culture and objectives. A consequence of integration is usually the loss of creativity because employees have to adhere to corporate guidelines, which do not generally leave much room for deviation and freedom.

Decentralization gives employees a great deal more autonomy and decision power, which generally leads to increased creativity. The risk here, though, is that the organization will be unable to share data, knowledge and know-how or best practices because the IT system may not support it or, as is often the case, because each department works in isolation and does not communicate with the others.

> When LEGO decided to invest in big data and integrate its digital strategy as part of its business strategy, the company faced an important dilemma. Should it move toward a more integrated data management system that would support knowledge transfer but would also affect creativity, speed and innovation? Or should it stick with its fragmented structure and accept the constraints as part of the game? The answer was not easy. Both options had their pros and cons. Having the profit formula in mind would help it remain focused and avoid becoming dispersed.

Whether your company deliberately chooses to embrace the digital era and proactively develop a corporate digital strategy or whether it merely joins the train to avoid being left behind, it will encounter a similar dilemma and will need to reflect on and evaluate the pros and cons of each scenario. Companies for which creativity is not a priority will most likely opt for an integrated approach. Those

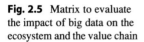

Fig. 2.5 Matrix to evaluate
the impact of big data on the
ecosystem and the value chain

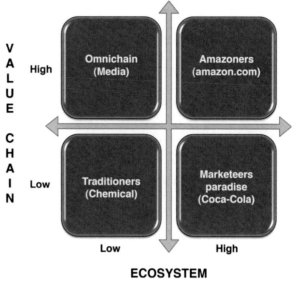

wishing to preserve the organization's entrepreneurial spirit are more likely to adopt a more autonomous structure at the expense of greater integration. Every case is different and will have its own answer.

2.3.3 Potential Scenarios

One way to facilitate the decision-making process is to develop several potential scenarios to evaluate where the company might stand in each case, and then design a portfolio of strategies for each of them.

Figure 2.5 presents an example of a matrix defined by two drivers: (1) the impact of big data on the **ecosystem**, and (2) the impact of big data on the **value chain**.

The purpose of the matrix is to clarify how the impact of big data on these two drivers will affect the business model and profit formula. Analyzing in each case whether the impact will be high or low makes it possible to form a picture of what the future might be. The four scenarios are explained below.

Scenario A: The omnichain

- Ecosystem: Low impact
- Value chain: High impact

This scenario applies to companies whose value chain could benefit from the use of big data to become an omnichain. Healthcare company Mediq is a good example.

Its ecosystem has adapted but not been totally transformed. And yet, Mediq deliberately chose to change its business proposition, and its value chain was able to take advantage of big data and the change.

Thus, big data had a high impact on the company's business model and its profit formula.

Scenario B: The traditioners

- Ecosystem: Low impact
- Value chain: Low impact

This is a scenario that a chemical company might face. Big data may impact its ecosystem slightly in the way it communicates or interacts, as well as its value chain, but it will not call for a complete revision of the strategy because the existing one, if adapted to the new circumstances, will continue to be valid.

The impact on the company's profit formula and value chain will not be too high, as they will not go through major changes.

Scenario C: Marketers paradise

- Ecosystem: High impact
- Value chain: Low impact

Organizations that have a strong relationship with their consumers may see their communication channels change. They can create a new virtual world in parallel to their core business to enrich their value proposition without dramatically changing their business model or the way they make money. Good examples are fast-moving consumer goods companies such as soft-drink manufacturers. They will use the Internet to offer and tailor their products, to segment their customers, and so forth. They will adapt their corporate strategy to big data, but at the end of the day, the key experience for the consumer is to have a drink.

These companies will adapt new developments coming from new data to their value chain, which will not necessarily evolve toward an omnichain.

Their business model and profit formula will not change dramatically either as their company's main source of revenue will remain unchanged.

Scenario D: Amazoners

- Ecosystem: High impact
- Value chain: High impact

Some companies will discover that both their value chain and their ecosystem are completely changing due to the use of big data. Amazon's value chain completely metamorphosed from a traditional one to multiple personalized value chains serving different purposes. The integration of big data has affected its ecosystem in terms of its relationships with its customers, partners, suppliers and so forth.

Amazoners carry the big data concept in their genes, and their profit formula and business model has to be extensively re-worked to integrate all the changes.

2.3.4 New Thinking to Create New Models

We can see, then, that this evolution toward a blurry industry environment with no clear boundaries and rapid and unpredictable global changes is pushing companies to develop new models to create their strategies. Companies are part of an ecosystem that will be completely different in 5 years' time so they need to build the future business scenario that they think their company will experience. The portfolio of options approach can help design a company strategy.

In 2013 Malnight et al. proposed their two-directional thinking model ("view of the future and back") to help executives face this new reality. In a world of constant change where the pace of change is increasing and becoming more unpredictable, planning and predicting the future based on the past will no longer be feasible. Companies need to decide what future they want, and at the same time manage the short-term reality in a dynamic way.

Two-directional thinking is the solution to manage both realities simultaneously. The first direction is the usual one where you think from where you are at present toward where you want to be in the future. The second direction, which often happens at the same time, is to imagine how the future will be and look back toward the present to see what steps need to be taken to bring the company to the envisaged future.

2.4   The Example of LEGO

As we saw earlier in this chapter, prior to choosing which digital strategy to develop, and in order to get some feedback from its ecosystem to better understand how to play its cards, LEGO worked on four different initiatives[4]:

- Big data to interact with consumers
- Big data for more effective marketing
- Big data to ensure a common language
- Big data to reshape the business model.

---

[4] These four bullets refer to the information in Sect. 2.1.4. The complete LEGO case study is provided in Appendix 2 at the end of this chapter.

LEGO's actions show how the company was aware of its need to prepare for the big data revolution. But adapting to the new reality was not easy. It raised important dilemmas:

Business Scenario Before making any decisions, LEGO had to imagine the future scenario that it would be part of, otherwise, any strategy it embraced would be like groping in the dark. No company can afford to take such a high risk.

Strategic Options Based on its envisaged scenario, LEGO had to develop a portfolio of strategic options that it would have to play out to succeed. Those options might raise new dilemmas, such as whether to integrate the four initiatives into the same system and lose agility, or keep them in silos and lose information sharing.

Strategic Model LEGO then had to work out the best way to analyze the industry and develop a new business model to define and execute a corporate strategy that would ensure it succeeded in the scenario it had envisioned.

The first step in planning LEGO's company strategy was for its executives to imagine the business scenario 5 years down the line. The company could fit in the Marketers Paradise scenario, characterized by a huge impact on the company's ecosystem but low impact on its value chain. Which strategic analysis framework should LEGO use to design its corporate strategy? We think that, with two-directional thinking in mind, it should review its portfolio of options and select initiatives that strengthen its marketing and customer interaction areas.

There is no right or wrong solution in this case. LEGO's dilemma was complex and all of the options had their pros and cons. Many companies will probably have to undergo a similar exercise in the near future and this case is a good example of the types of problems that leaders will need to reflect upon in preparation for that moment.

2.5 Deciding on the Best Strategy for Your Company

Having taken your company through the journey described in this chapter, you should already have a fairly clear idea about how big data will affect your overall corporate strategy. The change will not *necessarily* be dramatic. You may decide that your company either:

1. Does not need a digital strategy
2. Needs to incorporate a digital strategy into its corporate strategy
3. Should make its corporate strategy digital.

2.5.1   The Digital Fit: No Need for a Digital Strategy

If your company serves only a few customers and the information that big data usually provides is not relevant to any of its processes or its value chain, then it probably will not need a digital strategy and will not need to make major changes to its corporate strategy to include big data. However, this chapter proposes an evolution in the way companies look at their strategy, and this is valid regardless of the impact of big data on them.

A chemical company that has only a few suppliers and a mission to make chemical components to be sold to a small number of customers will not depend on the evolution of big data. Its success will be based on traditional aspects (price, quality, distribution, partnerships, etc.).

2.5.2   The Digital Masterplan: Digital Strategy as Part of the Corporate Strategy

Your company may discover that it needs to incorporate a digital strategy because the use of big data will be important for it to remain competitive but that it will not be its core strategy or business. The marketing function will probably benefit from big data elements such as sentiment analysis as well as consumer behavior, preferences and patterns to get to know customers better and reach them more efficiently by tailoring messages to different targets and using the most appropriate communication channels.

Organizations like Coca-Cola might position themselves in this category. These companies can take advantage of big data and social networks to market their products and communicate with their customers, but at the end of the day, it all comes down to the physical experience of consuming products such as soft drinks.

2.5.3   Digital DNA

If your company would not survive without the digital aspects and if big data is part of everything it does, including its value chain, distribution, communication and so forth, then digital is clearly part of its DNA.

Insurance company Axa uses big data to form a better picture of risk. It has completely transformed its business, including the way its brokers work, the solutions the company offers its clients, and the way it collects information from them. Big data has impacted Axa's entire structure and strategy.

Car insurance companies that have developed the "pay as you drive" concept are also transforming the way they calculate and implement an insurance product. They are changing the car insurance concept and its operating rules.

2.6 Conclusions

In this chapter we first analyzed how the digital world has been evolving and affecting companies in different ways.

The **omnichannel** reflects new consumer behaviors whereby shoppers combine different channels, both virtual and physical, to make a purchase. Shopping is transformed into a new experience, far richer than just acquiring a product.

The **omnichain** is a modular value chain made of interchangeable units that can be reconfigured in real time to deliver products and services at an almost individual level to meet the specific needs of customers. The omnichain has not yet reached its full potential, but this can be envisaged looking at how some new innovative businesses organize their processes.

Digital fusion is the outcome of merging physical and virtual realities and integrating them into the company's core. This is the direction in which our world is going. Not all companies will end up integrating digital fusion as part of their core business, but many will experience it as a life-threatening change that will require immediate action.

We also saw that embracing the big data era implies defining a digital strategy. This requires first understanding what a digital strategy is and what parts of the company it will impact, then figuring out how to go about defining it. New business model generation frameworks are needed for this exercise because those that have been used for the last three decades or more are unsuited to today's context of rapidly changing business ecosystems. In fact, the context has already changed dramatically since some of the more recent strategic models now being used were proposed.

We looked at some of the main business model streams to understand which ones would be best suited to a digital strategy. Two-directional thinking was one of them. This involves preparing for the future while managing the present, for example by envisioning future scenarios and directing the company toward the one that seems most likely to become real.

Two-directional thinking will also help in selecting the main criteria to be used in developing a portfolio of options and in choosing and implementing the best options from that matrix at any given moment. The final objective is always to be able to adapt to the current reality while staying on the right path to succeed in the envisioned future scenario.

Throughout the chapter, we have used a variety of examples to illustrate the different strategies and business models discussed. Some, like Google and Amazon, were born in the digital era and master the use of big data. However, this book is not about them. It is about how traditional industry sectors and companies like Axa, Mediq, LEGO, Coca-Cola and others that have been around for decades will be affected by the use of big data and must now re-adapt to a new reality in which big data occupies a predominant place. During this process, they will face major dilemmas such as choosing between integration and autonomy. This will push them to rethink their strategy and determine which direction to take.

Big data may not bring about a profound change in every company, but it is changing the way we are all doing business. Small changes can produce huge effects. The use of big data will slowly modify the way we understand business, and it will generate a silent revolution that will most likely redefine corporate business.

Appendix 1

The Evolution of the Corporate Strategy

This appendix provides additional information about some key business trends not discussed in the chapter.

Blue Ocean Strategy

This concept first appeared in 2005 (Kim and Mauborgne 2005). In a world of fierce competition, this model proposed to focus on untapped new markets in which to grow the company. Unlike red oceans, which refer to an ecosystem swarming with blood-thirsty rivals, blue oceans represented undiscovered territory with new market niches void of competitors.

Many companies took advantage of such opportunities. Uber was one of them. Many other successful companies like Apple and Google were not the first ones in their ocean yet they still managed to be highly successful. And companies that did create their own blue ocean, soon saw the ocean turn red as other organizations copied—and sometimes improved on—their original idea. So while this strategy can allow a company to make a U-turn in the way it operates or create a new brand from scratch, it does not offer a strategy for the long term.

Blurring Industry Boundaries

In 2013 Professor Thomas Malnight et al. published a book based on interviews of more than 150 CEOs and global leaders (Malnight et al. 2013). The goal was to offer insights and practical tools for leaders to prepare their businesses, and themselves, for the future.

One of the conclusions was that fundamental trends are reshaping the business landscape. For example industry boundaries are blurring, or even falling, and the expectations—or demands—of consumers, employees and even society as a whole are changing. Consumers have become much more proactive. They want to be listened to and be influential, and they expect organizations to react to their feedback.

To survive in this new landscape, Malnight proposed a two-directional thinking model that involves looking into the long term to define the company's major strategic foundation while focusing on the short term to adapt the strategy to the current reality. This two-directional thinking requires leaders to reassess their playing field to form a clear-eyed view of the world around them. It also requires them to redefine their ambition as a basis for building a long-term agenda. While no one can predict the future with certainty, developing an informed point of view of how the future might look and what it will take to be successful is the critical foundation for leaders today.

In preparing for the future, leaders need to understand the new reality by observing it and analyzing it on its own terms as well as throwing away the old ways of operating. Boundaries are falling, "giving way to complex, connected ecosystems that are more like webs than a collection of boxes" (Malnight et al. 2013). Competition can come from unrelated fields and is no longer centered on what a company produces but on what consumers want, which again changes the playing field.

View of the Future and Back

Once we know the "why" of our company, we need to go back to Malnight's model and prepare for the long term, bearing in mind that change is constant and that the pace of change is increasing and becoming more unpredictable, which means that planning and predicting the future based on the past we know is no longer going to work. Companies need to make up their mind about the future they want, and at the same time manage the short-term reality in a dynamic way.

Planning the long-term future while managing the short-term reality is not easy. Often managers remain stuck in the short term as they respond to the intense pressure from various outside players to deliver immediate results, thereby ignoring the future they had planned.

Two-directional thinking is the solution to manage both realities at the same time. The first direction is the usual one, where thinking goes from where you are in the present toward where you want to be in the future; the second direction, which often happens in parallel, requires leaders to imagine how the future will be and where they will be standing and, from there, look back to the present to see what steps are needed to reach the future they want to be part of.

Appendix 2: IMD Case LEGO

IMD-7-1644
01.04.2015

LEGO: DEFINING ITS ROUTE THROUGH BIG DATA

Researcher Teresa Ferreiro prepared this case under the supervision of Professor Carlos Cordón as a basis for class discussion rather than to illustrate either effective or ineffective handling of a business situation.

BILLUND, DENMARK, LEGO HEADQUARTERS. 12 OCTOBER 2014. Claus Pejstrup, finance SVP and leader of LEGO's journey toward big data, was about to attend an important meeting. The new corporate path toward big data would be decided in the meeting.

LEGO had started its journey toward big data years earlier, launching a number of initiatives within the company. Some had to do with the final consumer, others were more product and operations oriented. They were like independent islands in the ocean. Claus had recently been appointed to lead that journey and one of his major short-term challenges was to find some answers: Should the company keep supporting these siloed, unconnected initiatives, or should it foster only one broad, cross-cutting initiative? Whatever the decision, the company's resources were not endless, and using big data could cause big losses if the investments were too high and the return low.[1] At LEGO, a single big initiative would be much more expensive than the smaller ones and much riskier, yet it would potentially be much more effective as all the information would be centralized.

In a world in which every company, every website, every electronic device was sending and collecting data about anything and everything – behaviors, sentiments, health decisions and more – LEGO could not stand still. The penetration of smart phones had exploded from 5% of the global population in 2009 to 22% in 2013,[2] and to 66.8% of the population in the US by January 2014.[3] By analyzing big data, LEGO could better understand which product a person would buy after acquiring The Arctic Expedition from LEGO City, say. Or which promotions were more successful, or the preferences of Portuguese children between 7 and 10 years old. Big data could be a useful forecasting tool, as well as helping establish a direct communication line with customers and consumers via social media.

But LEGO was a family company, and decisions had always been made based mainly on experience and gut feeling. The final word was often driven by the intuition of the key executives. This was how LEGO had recovered from a serious crisis, to become the number two toy company in the world in September 2014. So why change anything? Claus urgently needed to set priorities and stick to them in order to define LEGO's big data strategy. But what to do, and how?

Company Background

The LEGO Group was established in 1932 by Ole Kirk Kristiansen in his carpenter shop in Billund, Denmark. For almost 70 years it saw steady growth in both sales and profits until, in 1998, this successful streak came to an abrupt end and the company started losing money. Staff reductions followed for the first time in its history, and LEGO set out on a path of innovative new product development.

By the end of 2002 the company appeared to have turned the corner, but 2004 exceeded even the company's own worst expectations. With sales having dropped 26% in 2003 alone and another 20% in 2004, LEGO faced bankruptcy. It was then that CEO Jørgen Vig Knudstorp, a young executive with a consulting background, built a survival plan that reversed the trend. From then on, LEGO kept growing to become the biggest toy company in the world by 2014. Asked what had made this possible, CFO John Goodwin said that during this time LEGO had focused on creating a great play experience for kids, with 60% of its product line new every year.[4] Also playing an important role in the company's success were the four pillars of its strategy: (1) expanding its global presence, (2) leveraging digitalization, (3) sustaining core commercial and operational momentum, and (4) creating the organization of the future.[5]

The Physical and Digital Landscape

In 2014 LEGO's powerful place in the physical market was not enough for it to sustain its leadership. Kids had many other interests apart from building bricks, so if the company wanted to keep its number one position, it needed to improve its presence in other business areas, mainly the digital scene.

> Kids don't make the distinction between the digital and the non-digital like those of us who weren't brought up in the digital age. For them it's all just one experience.[6]
>
> John Goodwin, CFO[7]

Over the previous two years, a revolution had taken place in the digital game world as Minecraft, a digital game made by an industry outsider, became the best-selling video game of all time in February 2014, with 42 million units sold.[8] The mission was to build worlds in a given space, using a set of tools that were either provided at the beginning of the game or collected by users as they played. Its creator was a Swedish programmer who developed it almost for the fun. "I'm not an entrepreneur, […] I'm not a CEO. I'm a nerdy computer programmer who likes to have opinions on Twitter,"[9] he said to describe himself.

In a way, it would have made sense for LEGO to invent Minecraft. Both games shared the same mission: to build worlds with bricks, Minecraft in virtual space, LEGO in physical space. But the truth is that LEGO would never have released such a game, with its pixelated style that made it look unfinished or technologically old. LEGO video games used high-definition resolution to show LEGO bricks and figures as they actually looked.

Consumers are not predictable. Nobody would have forecast that a game with such an old, unfinished look would become a blockbuster. But it did. It became the new challenge for eight-year-old kids.

LEGO reacted with what it does best: a partnership in which LEGO built the physical Minecraft bricks and tools (refer to **Exhibit 1**). The combination was a hit that production had not foreseen, and stocks ran out immediately after release. In September 2014 Microsoft announced its acquisition of Mojang (Minecraft's maker) for a sum of $2.5 billion.[10]

- 3 -   IMD-7-1644

Other players like Disney and Nintendo had also entered the digital landscape with products that blended the digital and physical worlds and were in direct competition with the digital products developed by LEGO, such as LEGO FUSION, a system with four different products (LEGO FUSION Town Master, LEGO FUSION Battle Towers, LEGO FUSION Create & Race and LEGO FUSION Resort Designer) to satisfy the three sorts of games that kids usually play: tycooning, which involves building and managing, tower defense style games and racing[11] (*refer to* ***Exhibit 2***).

In fact, LEGO's core strategy for video games was mainly to attract players to play physically. Of course it wanted its games to be successful, but the key objective of developing them in the first place was to use them as a driver toward the physical bricks. That was LEGO's identity and what made it so strong.

> Physical creation is something that's just wired inside all of us, and the joy you get from that can't fully be replicated via a virtual experience.
>
> John Goodwin[12]

What Exactly Is Big Data?

The first step toward including big data in the company's overall business strategy was to understand what it meant. Claus was very clear as he described big data and his expectations of it:

> "Big data" describes the ability to work with many data at the same time. But that does not bring anything to the company. Analytics is the ability to analyze and manage big data, thus finding valuable connections that you had not thought about before. You can't do it "humanly" but thanks to the new technologies we will be able to see new patterns that we did not have access to before.

Gartner had already defined big data as "high-volume, -velocity and -variety information assets that demand cost-effective, innovative forms of information processing for enhanced insight and decision making."[13] This definition, with its three *V*s, quickly became the standard definition. Later on, fourth and fifth *V*s, and the ones that many experts claimed to be most relevant, were added: *veracity* and *value*. Because if this huge amount of data was useless, what was the point of collecting it? The patterns revealed in the analysis of big data, and a company's ability to take decisions based on those insights, were what gave big data value (*for more information refer to* ***Appendix 1***).

Looking Inside LEGO

LEGO had been working hard on the implementation and use of big data in different areas of the company through several projects and initiatives (*refer to* ***Exhibit 3***). It was a great opportunity for the company to get to know its consumers better, to learn their patterns and preferences in order to market to them more effectively. Knowing its customers would help LEGO improve its sales predictions and demand planning. Further down the value chain, distribution, manufacturing and sourcing could also obtain great benefits from using big data.

Of the various initiatives undertaken by LEGO, four main projects were very visible at top management level: (1) the Business Intelligence Concept Foundation (BICF), the biggest and most important one, developed to create a new business world solution to find a common definition of data within the company, to enable much stronger standard reporting and provide a data repository for big data; (2) the HORIZON program to fully integrate the value chain planning, securing effective execution; (3) the Marketing Effectiveness (MRME) and Customer Planning System (GCPS) to improve marketing effectiveness, customer planning and trade marketing planning; and (4) the ecosystem project, to combine all digital platforms in one single user experience.

Bringing High-level Consistency to Data: The BICF

To get ready for big data, in 2012 LEGO took on the great challenge of what it called the BICF (Business Intelligence Concept Foundation), whose main objective was to achieve standardization data-wise. Until then data was stored centrally but handled locally by the various business units, which created reports following guidelines provided by their direct leader rather than by corporate standards. These were often were very time-consuming and useless reports that served the purpose of just one person. In addition, users accessing the system could pull up a report from the data they selected based on their own interpretation, which resulted in a loss of rigor and trustworthiness. It was necessary to put the existing data in order and give them more value by creating standard reports available to all business units. At the time, the equivalent of nearly 500 full-time employees (FTEs) globally were devoted just to generating reports. If these reports had been defined and standardized from the top, most of these FTEs could be reallocated to the analytical task of studying the information and coming up with ideas and suggestions of how to use it.

The challenges in the BICF project were that executives had become used to having their "own" reports, which they believed presented the information in the best way for them to make decisions and add value to the organization. Thus, reaching an agreement about the proper definition of particular data goes against what every executive believes is the best for their own job. For example, the definition of sales varies for different people. Some are used to having sales represent the total sales figure, while others believe that the sales figure should be net of discounts offered to retailers.

To make things more complicated, the people who were creating reports manually were not easily going to accept the standardization, since it meant that part of their job would be in danger.

Processing Company Information throughout the Value Chain: The HORIZON Project

HORIZON was born out of a desire to match LEGO's IT with the way it operated as a company. When HORIZON started, a lot of work had already been done to establish an integrated value chain based on a physical infrastructure to support it. Also, the global operating principles had been defined.

The full execution of this strategic direction was, however, limited by the IT set-up designed and implemented many years previously. But the new business landscape was much more diverse. There was a fast-changing retail landscape that included on the one hand the addition of new markets, and on the other the digitalization of the play experience. This evolution transformed the whole value chain but the IT system had not yet adapted to it. LEGO ran on SAP, an IT-integrated model that brought together all the company information in a big database. Its main constraint was that the present SAP set-up was designed for a different business reality. To compensate for this discordance LEGO needed to rely on manual interventions, many Excel sheets and customization to the system.

IMD   - 5 -   IMD-7-1644

Maarten Tibosch, SVP value chain innovation, commented:

> SAP as a system is not the issue. It is how we use it to support running LEGO as one integrated machine.

The HORIZON project tried to resolve the situation. It also acknowledged the need for flexibility to improve responsiveness.

Processing Data from Consumers: The MRME and GCPS Initiatives

LEGO classified its consumers by age in three groups: older, from 9 to 11; younger, from 5 to 8; and pre-school, from 2 to 3. Adults were also targeted in all marketing actions, especially those aimed at pre-school. The toy industry had strict regulations for protecting children, and very often parental supervision was required. In addition, it was usually adults who bought the game, even though from 5 years onwards, the child usually had the decision power.

Only by knowing its consumers well could the company target them effectively. Among the initiatives LEGO put in place to collect consumer information were traditional ones such as call centers, local events, and the *Club Magazine*, a paper magazine that reached 2 million children. Some new sources added complexity to the scene. Online companies well known for being heavy big data users, such as Amazon, provided LEGO with the data that related to their users and what they did. LEGO, on its side, devoted a small group of analysts to look through these data in search of opportunities and new ideas.

Big data was already helping the company target consumers in a number of ways:

- In the area of media planning, big data helped the company improve the effect of campaigns. It could target its promotions better and address them only to potential consumers. For example, before it used big data, LEGO would advertise pre-school products on TV knowing that around 70% of the audience were not potential consumers. By collaborating with cable providers that used big data, LEGO was able to improve its demographic information and thus narrow down and reach only the households with small kids that it was initially targeting. In the future LEGO knew that the natural evolution of these tools would allow it to develop micro-marketing, customized to local markets or very specific segments.

- Marketing effectiveness also benefited from the use of big data. LEGO was working with a multinational consulting company to analyze big data to better understand which parts of its marketing mix were more successfully hitting the right targets and which were not. It learned, for example, that TV was still the most important element in the company's marketing mix, although it was much more fragmented in a variety of children's channels than before. Also, digital TV was gaining importance for the segment of older kids who already had access to the internet without parental control. Big data also helped LEGO improve its knowledge of the impact and effectiveness of social media among its different targets.

A missed opportunity was that all the learning acquired by MRME and GCPS was not transferred to forecasting. Eventually, such a transfer would lead to better forecasts and, therefore, a much better supply chain service and effectiveness.

Bringing Together All Digital Platforms for the User: The Ecosystem

For most of its physical products, LEGO at some point created its own digital experience so it could interact with users, e.g. a Facebook page, Twitter account, mobile app, etc. As a result, the LEGO digital experience was fragmented and dissolved in the global digital world. Consumers often felt overwhelmed and frustrated at having to register again and again for LEGO's siloed applications. It was also discouraging for LEGO to see that the information that the units were collecting was not shared; there was no central database to collect all the data and leverage it for the rest of the company either. So eventually, as valuable as it was, the collected data reached a dead end and were never used.

The ecosystem (*refer to **Exhibit 4***) was a new initiative created with the objective of taking all consumer digital platforms and combining them into a single consumer experience. As it was conceived, it would be beneficial for both consumer and company. For consumers, it would create a richer experience, connecting all the dots of their LEGO world; for the company, it would centralize all the information about each user, improving the database and making it easier to handle the consumer data. As a result, LEGO would have a happier consumer who would be closer and more loyal to the brand.

LEGO liked to compare its digital path to the one Apple had walked years earlier when it had launched the iPhone. At that time, Apple had great physical products like the Mac and iPhone itself. Over time, it built some digital elements such as iTunes or the Apple Store to connect and enhance its digital products. Likewise, LEGO also initially offered only its physical bricks. At some point it had created a few fragmented experiences that would now evolve toward a common connected world.

This project was expected to be launched in two phases between 2015 and 2016.

Decision Dilemmas

At the upcoming meeting in Billund, the challenge for top management was to decide which of all the initiatives around big data to support in the future. Should it adopt a totally integrated approach, ensuring that all projects would fit perfectly with one another, or at the other extreme, should each project be totally independent, prove its own business case and follow a Darwinian approach in which the only the best adapted would survive?

In respect of the BCIF project, had the company and its employees understood that the foundational project was the basis that had to be implemented so that the rest of initiatives could happen? If not, what actions should be taken to push it forward and break internal resistance?

Was it worth investing in the HORIZON project? Would there be a return on investment, or would it be better to keep the status quo, relying on the human talent to make the system work? Would such a project mean the death of the common integrated SAP platform and give way to a series of operating systems that would not be compatible with one another?

And what about the consumer-related initiatives? Was big data the future that all companies were keen to embrace, or was it a fad that would go away? The potential of big data was certainly huge, but did LEGO want to invest in something that would not bring the company much more than a modern image? Right now, the knowledge from both MROS and the ecosystem was not being communicated to the forecasting and demand planning departments. So in a way, the potential of big data was lost due to a fragmented structure.

Should LEGO walk toward a more integrated data management system that would support knowledge transfer but would also affect creativity, speed and innovation? Or should it remain with the fragmented structure that it had today, accepting its constraints as part of the game? If the company decided to invest in big data, were these the right initiatives to support? Too many initiatives were in the development process. How to move forward? Claus wondered…

Appendix 1
About Big Data

Where Does Big Data Come From?

Building on the initial definition, without taking into consideration the fourth and fifth *Vs* – *veracity and value*, big data could be divided by the types of devices from which it is generated, which are mainly (1) personal devices such as smartphones, tablets and personal computers, (2) wearable devices, and (3) the Internet of Things.

The adoption of smart phones by the general public, which took off in 2009,[14] allowed users to generate all kinds of data anytime, anywhere. This, combined with the expansion of social media, which made it so easy to post and share content on the web directly from a smart phone, fostered the growth of big data. A little later, in 2010, the Internet of Things (IoT), which refers to the data generated by physical devices that are connected and accessed through the web,[15] gained momentum and within a year was producing roughly as much data as all personal devices.[16] Where did the IoT come from, and why in 2010? According to Cisco, the IoT was born around 2008 and 2009, the inflexion point at which the number of gadgets connected to the network exceeded the number of people on earth.[17] Today, predictions show that by 2018 they will double the amount of data generated by the other two groups together. By 2020 the IoT will create $1.9 trillion of economic value add.[18] Almost every device has a sensor today, and every sensor collects data that is part of the IoT.

Two ways in which these types of data could generate value for organizations are: (1) by enabling companies to gain a better understanding of their consumers and to target them more effectively and help to predict sales; and (2) in a more functional way, by helping to transform the business or improve business processes.

Exhibit 1
LEGO Minecraft

Source: http://www.LEGO.com

Exhibit 2
LEGO FUSION Town Master: A Game that Combines Physical and Digital Experience

Source: http://www.LEGO.com. More information about LEGO FUSION can be obtained from http://www.lego.com/en-us/fusion

Exhibit 3
LEGO Value Chain: LEGO Initiatives

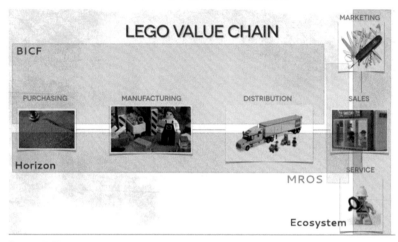

Source: IMD team

Exhibit 4
The Ecosystem

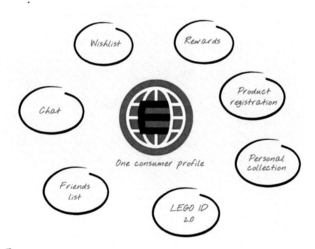

Source: LEGO

References

[1] Visibelly, Marco. "How Big Data Can Mean Big Money — or Big Losses." Wired, 13 August 2014. http://www.wired.com/2014/08/big-data-can-mean-big-money-big-losses/ <accessed 21 January 2015>.

[2] Heggestuen, John. "One in Every 5 People in the World Own a Smartphone, One in Every 17 Own a Tablet." Business Insider, 15 December 2013. http://www.businessinsider.com/smartphone-and-tablet-penetration-2013-10 <accessed 21 January 2015>.

[3] "Smartphone Penetration Now at Two-Thirds of the US Mobile Market". Marketing Charts, 10 March 2014. http://www.marketingcharts.com/online/smartphone-penetration-now-at-two-thirds-of-the-us-mobile-market-41248/ <accessed 21 January 2015>.

[4] Petroff, Alanna. "Lego becomes world's biggest toymaker." CNN, 4 September 2014. http://money.cnn.com/2014/09/04/news/companies/LEGO-biggest-toymaker/ <accessed 21 January 2015>.

[5] The LEGO group – a short presentation 2014. LEGO, 10 June 2014. http://www.lego.com/en-gb/aboutus/media-library#?filter&ids=338e7888a00c4b6abb7e811e50870271 <accessed 21 January 2015>.

[6] Hansegard, Jens. "Oh, Snap! Lego's Sales Surpass Mattel" The Wall Street Journal, 4 September 2014. http://online.wsj.com/articles/LEGO-becomes-worlds-largest-toy-maker-on-movie-success-1409820074 <accessed 21 January 2015>.

[7] For more information, see LEGO's internal video: "Transformative Changes for Young People at Play", 17 May 2013. https://LEGOexternal.23video.com/v.ihtml?source=share&photo%5fid=7547661 <accessed 21 January 2015>.

[8] Burke, Steve. "Minecraft Is The Most-Selling Video Game of All Time at 42 Million Units", Gamers Nexus, 4 February 2014. http://www.gamersnexus.net/news/1308-minecraft-most-selling-game-all-time#GQIPieiTCEqvfuMS.99http://www.gamersnexus.net/news/1308-minecraft-most-selling-game-all-time <accessed 21 January 2015>.

[9] Ewing, Adam. "Minecraft creator moves on from Mojang." Stuff. http://www.stuff.co.nz/technology/games/61304952/minecraft-creator-moves-on-from-mojang.

[10] Ovide, Shira. "Microsoft Gets 'Minecraft'—Not the Founders." The Wall Street Journal, 15 September 2014. http://www.wsj.com/articles/microsoft-agrees-to-acquire-creator-of-minecraft-1410786190 <accessed 21 January 2015>.

[11] Lee, Nicole. "Lego Fusion lets you build virtual playgrounds with real-world bricks." Engadget, 19 June 2014. http://www.engadget.com/2014/06/19/lego-fusion/ <accessed 21 January 2015>.

[12] Gustafsson, Katarina. "Rebuilding Lego for Today's Kids." Bloomberg Business Week, 7 November 2013. http://www.businessweek.com/articles/2013-11-07/LEGO-launches-toys-more-complex-than-blocks-fit-for-digital-age <accessed 21 January 2015>.

[13] Sicular, Svetlana. "Gartner's Big Data Definition Consists of Three Parts, Not to Be Confused with Three "V"s". Forbes 27 March 2013. http://www.forbes.com/sites/gartnergroup/2013/03/27/gartners-big-data-definition-consists-of-three-parts-not-to-be-confused-with-three-vs/ <accessed 21 January 2015>.

[14] "The Growth of Mobile Users and Mobile SEO. The Cold Hard Data On Smartphones." Online Specialists, 7 May 2013. http://www.onlinespecialists.com.au/the-growth-of-mobile-users-and-mobile-seo/ <accessed 21 January 2015>.

[15] "M2M World of Connected Services. The Internet of Things." Beecham Technology Partners. http://beechamtech.com/?page_id=47 <accessed 21 January 2015>.

[16] Danova, Tony. "The Internet of Everything: 2014 [Slide Deck]." Business Insider. http://www.businessinsider.com/the-internet-of-everything-2014-slide-deck-sai-2014-2?op=1 <accessed 21 January 2015>.

[17] Evans, Dave. "The Internet of Things. How the Next Evolution of the Internet Is Changing Everything" Cisco IBSG, April 2011

- 12 -   IMD-7-1644

http://www.cisco.com/web/about/ac79/docs/innov/IoT_IBSG_0411FINAL.pdf <accessed 21 January 2015>.

[18] "Gartner Says Personal Worlds and the Internet of Everything Are Colliding to Create New Markets." Press release. Barcelona, Spain, 11 November 2013. http://www.gartner.com/newsroom/id/2621015 <accessed 21 January 2015>.

References

Aamoth, Doug. 2013. 50 best iPhone apps, 2013 edition. Time, September 17. http://techland.time.com/2013/09/20/50-best-iphone-apps-2013-edition/slide/uber/. Accessed August 7, 2015.

ATKearney. 2014. On solid ground: Brick-and-mortar is the foundation of omnichannel retailing. https://www.atkearney.com/documents/10192/4683364/On+Solid+Ground.pdf/f96d82ce-e40c-450d-97bb-884b017f4cd7. Accessed August 7, 2015.

Axa. 2014. AXA creates broker "big data" tool to provide greater customer insight and market competitiveness. Axa press release, November 13. http://www.axa.co.uk/newsroom/media-releases/2014/axa-creates-broker-big-data-tool-to-provide-greater-customer-insight-and-market-competitiveness/. Accessed August 7, 2015.

Bradshaw, Tim. 2014. Uber valued at $40bn in latest funding round. Financial Times. December, 4. http://www.ft.com/intl/cms/s/0/66a76576-7bdc-11e4-a7b8-00144feabdc0.html#axzz3U00kVFAO. Accessed August 7, 2015.

Büchel, Bettina, James Henderson, and Cyril Bouquet. 2011. Leading strategic initiatives in an era of uncertainty: When to commit to action, Insights@IMD No. 2. IMD.

Butera, Steve, and Mike Donila. 2015. More malls in the U.S. in "dying status." WBIR.com, January 30. http://www.wbir.com/story/news/local/2015/01/30/more-malls-in-the-us-in-dying-status/22558297/. Accessed August 7, 2015.

Cord, David J. 2014. The decline and fall of Nokia. Schildts & Söderströms.

Cordón, Carlos and Teresa Ferreiro. 2015. LEGO: Defining its route through big data. IMD case study no. IMD-7-1644.

Damodaran, Aswath. 2014. A disruptive cab ride to riches: The Uber payoff. Forbes, October 6. http://www.forbes.com/sites/aswathdamodaran/2014/06/10/a-disruptive-cab-ride-to-riches-the-uber-payoff/. Accessed August 7, 2015.

Earnest, Leslie. 2002. Nike buys softwear titan Hurley. Los Angeles Times, February 22.

eMarketer. 2014. Retail sales worldwide will top $22 trillion this year. December, 23. http://www.emarketer.com/Article/Retail-Sales-Worldwide-Will-Top-22-Trillion-This-Year/1011765. Accessed August 7, 2015.

Everett, Dan. 2012. Governance: The big data elephant in the room. Forbes, December 6.

Killing, Peter. 2003. Nestlé's Globe program (A): The early months. IMD case no. IMD-3-1335; Nestlé's Globe program (B): July executive board meeting. IMD case no. IMD-3-1335; Nestlé's Globe progam (C): "Globe Day." IMD case no. IMD-3-1336, IMD.

Kim, W. Chan, and Renee Mauborgne. 2005. Blue ocean strategy: How to create uncontested market space and make competition irrelevant. Harvard Business School Press.

LEGO. (n.d.) LEGO Fusion. http://www.lego.com/en-us/fusion. Accessed August 7, 2015.

Malnight, Thomas. 2007. Cascading must-win battles at Carlsberg. A textbook case in corporate turnaround. IMD, July. http://www.imd.org/research/challenges/upload/cascading_must_win_battles_at_Carlsberg.pdf. Accessed August 10, 2015.

Malnight, Thomas, Tracey Keys, and Kees van der Graaf. 2013. Ready? The 3Rs of preparing your organization for the future. Strategy Dynamics Global SA.

Malnight, Thomas, Peter Killing, and Tracey Keys. 2006. Must-win battles: How to win them again and again. Halow (UK): Pearson Education Ltd.

Microsoft. 2012. The consumer journey: Global auto-buyers. Research conducted by Ipsos Media CT and Ipsos OTX, commissioned by Microsoft, February–June.

National Association of Insurance Commissioners. 2015. Usage-based insurance and telematics. NAIC and CIPR. April 24. http://www.naic.org/cipr_topics/topic_usage_based_insurance.htm. Accessed August 7, 2015.

Nike. 2012. Nike, Inc. to divest of Cole Haan and Umbro to focus on accelerating growth through Nike and complementary sport brands. Nike.com, Investors News Details, May 31. http://investors.nike.com/investors/news-events-and-reports/investor-news/investor-news-details/2012/NIKE-Inc-to-Divest-of-Cole-Haan-and-Umbro-to-Focus-on-Accelerating-Growth-Through-Nike-and-Complementary-Sport-Brands/default.aspx. Accessed August 10, 2015.

Nokia website. N.d. Our story. http://company.nokia.com/en/about-us/our-company/our-story. Accessed August 10, 2015.

Osterwalder, Alexander, and Yves Pigneur. 2010. Business Model Generation. A Handbook for Visionaries, Game Changers, and Challengers. John Wiley & Sons, Inc.

Peterson, Hayley. 2014. America's shopping malls are dying a slow, ugly death. BusinessInsider.com, January 31. http://www.businessinsider.com/shopping-malls-are-going-extinct-2014-1. Accessed August 7, 2015.

Porter, Michael. 1979. How competitive forces shape strategy. Harvard Business Review, March. https://hbr.org/1979/03/how-competitive-forces-shape-strategy/ar/1. Accessed August 7, 2015.

Rittman, Mark. 2006. Data profiling and automated cleansing using Oracle Warehouse Builder 10g release 2. Oracle website, September. http://www.oracle.com/technetwork/articles/rittman-owb-083421.html. Accessed July 2015.

Think with Google. 2014. New research shows how digital connects shoppers to local stores. October. https://www.thinkwithgoogle.com/articles/how-digital-connects-shoppers-to-local-stores.html. Accessed August 7, 2015.

Serialization in the Pharmaceutical Industry

3

Pharma is one of many industries where big data promises big changes. From accelerating the discovery and development of new drugs through optimizing the efficacy of clinical trials to gaining better insights into consumer behaviors, the list of potential applications is widely perceived to be really big!

Another development with potentially major implications in relation to big data is serialization, a new regulatory initiative that is steadily gaining momentum across the world. Serialization regulations in the pharmaceutical industry require a unique number to be assigned to each individual unit of saleable medicine. The

© Springer International Publishing Switzerland 2016   47
C. Cordon et al., *Strategy is Digital*, Management for Professionals,
DOI 10.1007/978-3-319-31132-6_3

main objective is to be able to detect counterfeit products and facilitate quality control as well as to increase visibility and traceability within the supply chain.

Serialization generates a massive amount of data that could be used to create a great deal of value for patients as well as for commercial entities involved in the discovery, production and delivery of medicines in the countries where this initiative has been implemented. Yet, to our surprise (and initial disappointment) we found little evidence, if at all, that pharmaceutical companies are seriously considering how to use serialization data to create value. The immediate concern of pharmaceutical companies has, so far, been on compliance. This is perhaps understandable, given the administrative burden and immense cost resulting from the serialization regulations.

We did nevertheless find one great example of a company that has successfully reinvented its business model as a result of sweeping changes in the healthcare industry. Dutch company Mediq has essentially redefined its business model from distributing pharmaceuticals to caring for patients by using big data and ensuring the integrity of the supply chain. Executives from the pharmaceutical industry can draw inspiration from Mediq's innovative approach to refocus their efforts from reactive compliance with regulations to proactive use of big data to create value once compliance has been achieved. Executives from other industries can also learn from Mediq's example how innovation in the face of adversity can deliver superior results.

In this chapter we start with a brief overview of pharmaceutical supply chains and serialization. We then examine the example of multinational pharmaceutical company Sanofi, which complied with new serialization policies in Turkey designed to safeguard the safety of the supply chain. Readers who are short of time or who are not interested in such details can go directly to the Mediq example in Sect. 3.7. We conclude with an exploration of the US healthcare market and the opportunities for value creation there from using big data.

3.1   Pharmaceutical Industry Supply Chains[1]

As in other industries, pharmaceutical companies have been under increasing pressure to deliver innovative high-quality products and services at competitive prices, so they have focused primarily on innovation. When it comes to achieving operational efficiencies, however, the business model of big pharma organizations has not changed in over two decades.

One strategy available to them is to reinvent their supply chains. Originally designed to produce large volumes using static manufacturing processes, pharmaceutical supply chains were mainly intended to comply with regulatory requirements and prevent running out of stocks, even though the cost of storing huge inventories was also high (Ehrhardt et al. 2012). In terms of performance in

---

[1] This section incorporates data and insights from Keeling et al. (2010).

inventory and capacity management, partner relations and supply chain efficiency, most pharma companies significantly lag behind consumer goods firms. On average, big pharma companies hold 258 days of inventory, close to four times more than the 72-day average in the consumer goods industry. The difference in manufacturing lead times between these two industries is even more staggering, 120–180 days in pharma vs. 3–7 days in the fast-moving consumer goods industry. While pharmaceuticals command higher margins than consumer goods, supply chain transformation in pharma companies could increase profits by approximately 10 % (Ebel et al. 2013).

A well-functioning supply chain is one designed to be flexible in terms of assets, suppliers, strategy, processes and talent. For example, segmentation in supply chains enables companies to focus on investments that are most likely to deliver the highest returns, which reduces the need for flexibility across various products and markets. Other measures, such as standardizing operational processes around lean order fulfillment and using forecasting for major product launches, help reduce variability. A company's ability to ramp production capacity up or down cost-effectively requires its assets to be fluid. This includes not only managing in-house production but also diversifying production to low-cost regions as well as acquiring and disposing of manufacturing assets. Moreover, following the example of other industries, big pharma companies have begun to trade capacity in order to balance supply and demand and generate savings.

As pharmaceutical supply chains have become more global and complex, managing the total cost of ownership means not only negotiating favorable terms with suppliers and ensuring their flexibility but also constantly innovating to meet fluctuating demand. Flexibility and cost management have become especially relevant with the rise of generic drugs and the practice among successful pharma companies of combining the production of specialized drugs and generics. Traditionally, big pharma companies have priced their products using a value-based approach, which is well suited for patented products, whereas for generics a cost-plus pricing model allows companies to better estimate product profitability. However, traditional pharma companies do not have a clear understanding of the cost of goods sold at the individual product level and are therefore not always able to price their products competitively.

Big pharma companies also need to harmonize their products across different regulatory regimes in order to meet quality standards across the globe. Adopting the highest existing standard for all markets is often the most cost-effective strategy as it enables companies to pass scrutiny and stand prepared for the evolution of standards in less-developed markets in the future. As part of their compliance harmonization efforts, pharmaceutical industry players have joined forces to design an industry-wide supplier auditing system. With demand growing in emerging markets, the challenge for pharma companies has become even more complex, requiring not only flexibility and innovation but also a new approach to distribution, since the paths to the end customer differ across markets. For example, pharmaceutical companies in China have to deal with over a thousand multi-layered wholesalers, while in Brazil some have bypassed intermediaries altogether, forward-integrating distribution to gain a strategic advantage.

A flexible, dynamic supply chain that enables companies to ensure the quality and safety of their drugs and at the same time lower their operational costs is one that is supported by a well-designed information technology platform, as this is what will allow them to identify where most value is created and captured.

3.2   The Risk of Counterfeit Drugs

Pharmaceuticals have consistently ranked among the top 10 counterfeited goods, with product risk varying from market to market (Healthcare Packaging 2014). The possibilities offered by big data are now transforming pharmaceutical supply chains and allowing companies to manage risk by addressing serious problems related to theft, counterfeiting and diversion.

The World Health Organization describes a counterfeit medicine as being one that:

> [I]s deliberately and fraudulently mislabeled with respect to identity and/or source. Counterfeiting can apply to both branded and generic products, and counterfeit products may include products with the correct ingredients or with the wrong ingredients, without active ingredients, with insufficient active ingredients, or with fake packaging.
> World Health Organization (n.d.).

Counterfeit drugs account for around 1 % of medicines used in developed countries, and 30–40 % in developing countries (Manufacturing Chemist Pharma 2013), representing a total value of $75 billion to $200 billion and growing (Systech 2014). Fake medicines that are either inadequate or even toxic have led to harmful, and at times fatal, outcomes for the patients. This, in turn, undermines the reputation of major producers (Cockburn et al. 2005).

3.3   What Is Serialization?

Serialization is a method of assigning a unique number to every unit of a saleable product (see Fig. 3.1). The combination of serial numbers and an appropriate authentication process to validate products at each critical juncture in the supply chain provides visibility and full traceability throughout the supply chain, making it possible to control quality and detect counterfeits. Importantly, serialization requires all partners across the supply chain to collaborate to ensure that tracking is accurate and that data is properly managed as the product moves through the chain from manufacturing through distribution to the final point of sale (Cognizant 20–20 Insights 2013).

Although the upfront investment required to set up a mass serialization system to control the supply chain is substantial, in return pharmaceutical manufacturers

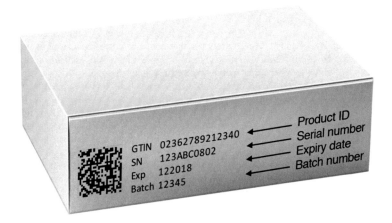

Fig. 3.1 Example of serialization on packaging

stand to benefit in terms of regulatory, financial and reputational risk protection. The system will allow them to identify counterfeit products and recall substandard drugs efficiently and promptly, thus ensuring patient safety and avoiding the risk of litigation and negative publicity, which can have a lasting damaging impact on the company's performance and shareholder return.

While the most obvious applications of mass serialization are preventing crime and mitigating the risks of patients being given the wrong medication, the data generated throughout the supply chain can also be exploited to improve the way medicines are used. A point-of-sale (POS) system that can scan and retrieve information about each pack of medicine could potentially free up pharmacists' time to provide patients with more information about their treatments in addition to dispensing the prescription.

3.4 Authentication and Track-and-Trace

Mass serialization technology can be used in two main ways: "authentication" and "track-and-trace." Authentication takes place at both ends of the supply chain, i.e., when a product enters it and when it exits it. This is the most cost-effective and easy-to-adopt method. However, it is less thorough than track-and-trace, which is a more complex system requiring validation at every step of the supply chain, which can amount to as many as 20 transactions.

The investment required to implement track-and-trace technologies for a single supply chain was estimated at €400 million in 2008, which at the time translated into an investment of €10 billion for the European Union as a whole. On top of this, operational costs were also projected to increase (Frost and Sulivan 2008).

On the face of it, this seems simple: Print a data matrix on each pack so it is readable, verify it, collect the data, and then hold it in a database to be able to export as required to regulators or other agencies. In reality, every step involved in achieving this goal requires complex systems to be added to an environment that is already complex in terms of systems and processes. It requires critical decisions to be taken—often on the basis of incomplete information—whose long-term impact may not be fully understood. Because every organization and its requirements are different, a one-size-fits-all solution is not available and the practicalities of implementation are fraught with difficulties. The buy-in of the company's senior stakeholders is essential for the significant resources for a complex, lengthy, and inevitably expensive project to be sanctioned. Focusing on the short-term "achieving compliance" outcomes is the typical approach, but this creates a defensive perspective. Being much clearer about additional benefits—including the potential for streamlining production and supply flows and adding greater visibility—is important. There seems to be little appetite for this, with the focus currently very much on license to operate, to the detriment of wider benefits that could be gained for everyone who has a stake in this sector: manufacturers, patients, healthcare professionals, payers, and society as a whole.

Christoph Krähenbühl, Managing Director, 3C Integrity (Healthcare Packaging 2014).

3.5   Adopting a Global Policy[2]

The effectiveness of mass serialization is dependent on all countries and stakeholders—including pharmaceutical companies, vendors and trade associations—adopting it. By 2017 serialization regulations are expected to cover over 70 % of global medicines. Compliance presents a complex challenge, because there is a great degree of variation between local regulations and there are currently no unified global standards. Therefore managing and implementing serialization requires not only a substantial financial investment but also an understanding of local markets and regulations. Turkey and China have well-established regulatory regimes in this area, but many other markets are still in the process in adopting regulations and ensuring compliance (Fig. 3.2).

The EU's Falsified Medicines Directive, which came into effect on January 2, 2013, introduced stricter rules to control the trade of medicines and ensure their safety in order to better protect public health. According to the European Commission Directorate-General for Taxation and Customs Union, over 30 million counterfeit medicines had been seized by customs officers at EU borders over the previous 5 years (European Commission 2011). The Directive imposed an obligatory authenticity feature on the outer packaging of the medicines; a common EU-wide logo to help distinguish legal online pharmacies from illegal ones; stricter inspections of producers of active pharmaceutical ingredients; and higher record-keeping requirements for wholesale distributors.

In the United States the Drug Quality and Security Act (DQSA) was signed into law by President Obama on November 27, 2013. It specified the necessary steps required for the creation of a secure electronic system to identify and trace certain

---

[2] This section incorporates data and insights from Healthcare Packaging (2014).

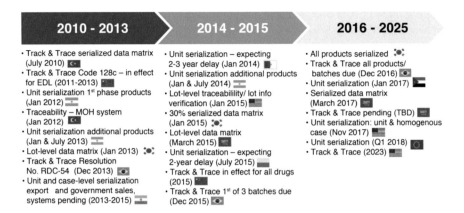

Fig. 3.2 Global regulatory landscape: Serialization/track-and-trace requirements (Adapted from Systech 2014)

prescription drugs circulating in the US market. The system had been designed to facilitate the exchange of information at the individual package level in order to verify the legitimacy of drugs and thus make it easier to detect illegitimate products and recall substandard products.

3.6   The Example of Turkey[3]

Against a backdrop of robust national economic growth, in 2012 Turkey's pharmaceutical market was the 6th largest in Europe and 16th largest in the world with $12.5 billion in sales. Its cumulative annual growth rate (CAGR) was nearly 10 % between 2003 and 2012. Moreover, R&D expenditure to manufacture basic pharmaceutical products grew at the staggering rate of 73 % from 2010 to 2011, surpassing $100 million in 2011. While multinational pharmaceutical players accounted for just over 30 % of the total Turkish market in 2012, local manufacturers such as Abdi İbrahim (7.5 %) and Bilim İlaç (~5 %) stood out from the fragmented pool of 300 pharmaceutical companies that together represented 44 % of the market.

Both domestic and international investments in the pharmaceutical sector ramped up given the country's ambitious targets for the healthcare industry and a new investment program launched in 2012 that identified pharmaceuticals as a priority area. Special attention was given to Free Healthcare Zones—designed to create economies of scale by establishing healthcare clusters—as well as to tax reductions of 15–65 % depending on the region, with numerous advantages for the public and manufacturers. In 2011 Turkey's public healthcare spending stood at

---

[3] This section incorporates data and insights from Deloitte and Investment and Support Promotion Agency (2014).

77 % (vs. 72 % OECD average), and most of the country's population of 72 million had access to healthcare services.

In order to operate in Turkey, pharma companies were required to have a license, which took on average 240 days to obtain, in accordance with the provisions of Turkish and EU legislation. Since January 1, 2010 all license holders in Turkey are obliged to add a track-and-trace code on all goods they manufacture so that these can be monitored at every stage in the process to prevent fraud and protect patients. The two-dimensional code includes:

- A barcode number, or Global Trade Item Number (GTIN), which comprises a maximum of 14 digits and is used to serialize products worldwide
- The serial number (SN), the unique registration number defined by the manufacturers for each unit/package on the basis of products
- The expiration date (XD), the last date at which the product can safely be used
- The batch number (BN), which distinguishes one batch from another during manufacturing.

The scope of Turkey's "Pharmaceuticals Track and Trace System" (ITS) covered all prescription drugs and medical nutrition products. Stakeholders included hospitals, physicians, pharmacies, manufacturers, importers, wholesalers and reimbursement institutions.

The ITS was rolled out in two phases. Phase 1 covered serialization of products sold in Turkey as of July 2010 by using a unique identifier on secondary packaging (including product code and serial number). In Phase 2, serialization and aggregation were implemented as of January 2012, with the Ministry of Health (MoH) and wholesalers receiving serial numbers of each and every box per invoice.

Serialization prevented counterfeit drugs in Turkish supply chain and both consumers and stakeholders were able to validate whether a product was counterfeit or not. Manufacturers that serialized their products could prevent economic damage caused by not only counterfeit drug production and sale, but also by fraudulent sales by their own representatives. Finally, serialization produced a valuable data about market demand, stock, and production forecasts. The most important challenge the manufacturers faced was adapting their production lines as well as their business logic to the requirements of the system, which had put an extra layer to the operation and product transportation between manufacturers and wholesalers. Since the system was designed for both public health and the manufacturers' own benefit, it was interesting to observe the manufacturers, who at first opposed the system, cooperating with it.

Taha Yayci, Consultant, Turkish Ministry of Health (Healthcare Packaging 2014)

Sanofi is one of the multinational pharma companies that implemented a serialization project in Turkey in accordance with the local regulatory requirements. In Phase 1, Sanofi could not find an experienced supplier to work with. It had to redesign the artwork on all its products and it experienced duplication and other errors due to software and sensor issues. As a result, in Phase 1, serialization had a minor impact on the overall equipment effectiveness (OEE) of about 1 %. Phase 2, however, was more costly and difficult to implement, especially given the tight regulatory timeline. The drop in OEE reached 15–25 % while additional operator support was required as a result of the increased workload. The company also dealt with distribution issues, which increased overtime and complexity in the product delivery and return processes, ultimately decreasing efficiency (Sanofi 2014).

Regardless of these challenges, Sanofi managed to serialize 55 million units in Phase 1; in Phase 2 it serialized and aggregated 70 million units out of the 340 million units it distributed overall. As a result, Sanofi found serialization and systematic controls at the pharmacy level to be highly beneficial for patient security and in its fight against reimbursement fraud. Another conclusion was that the aggregation phase was highly complex, costly and more difficult to implement. A tangible benefit for the company would have been to receive real-time data on the volumes of stocks available in the supply chain from the Turkish Ministry of Health.

Despite the potential value of the data collected, it remained largely unused because the rest of the supply chain (e.g., hospitals and pharmacies) was not equipped to deal with it. With about three billion boxes sold annually, each requiring approximately 14 actions to track its lifecycle, the data set comprised about 50 billion data points. As the data had to be kept for 12 years, this amounted to some 600 billion data points to be collected and stored. Using this massive amount of data presented a managerial rather than a technological challenge.

3.7 Mediq: A Leader in Value Chain Transformation[4]

Mediq is a Dutch healthcare company that used to be in the business of "moving boxes" as a distributor that purchased products from manufacturers and supplied them to customers either at home or through pharmacies. The use of big data enabled Mediq to transform its business model and become a leader in taking care of patients, setting a new standard for the pharmaceutical industry globally.

3.7.1 Changes in Dutch Legislation Focused on Reducing "HARM"

Mediq was prompted to critically review and evolve its business model following changes in Dutch legislation. In early 2012 the Dutch government faced the same demographic and socio-economic trends that were affecting the healthcare systems of its European neighbors. These trends included an ageing and growing population; an increase in incidences of chronic and complex illnesses; a heavier burden placed on primary and secondary care physicians; growing demand for early detection and prevention of illnesses; and a growing number of requests for advice from physicians about patients' health and well-being. To meet consumer demand within existing constraints and under price pressures, the emphasis in the

---

[4] This section includes information and insights from Mediq (2015).

pharmaceutical value chain began to shift from capturing product margins to a "fee-for-service" model.

To address avoidable healthcare costs of some €85 million annually as a result of incorrect use of medications leading to around 19,000 avoidable hospitalizations per year, the Dutch government introduced new policies focused on quality improvements in pharmacies. Minimizing hospital admissions related to medications (HARM) required improving compliance with guidelines in high-risk processes, with a particular focus on high-risk patients and providing solid support to prescribers of high-risk drugs (The Royal Dutch Pharmacists Association 2009). To this end, Mediq pharmacies developed an integrated pharmaceutical care program that provided insights into whether patients were using pharmaceuticals in an optimal manner.

Pharmacists and general practitioners decided together whether or not a patient was receiving the correct treatment, whether or not a patient was taking the medication correctly (therapy compliance), and whether or not the pharmaceutical treatment was in line with the most recent guidelines and scientific insights. A better-informed use of pharmaceuticals reduced the risk of treatment complications and unnecessary hospital admissions. The program was mainly intended for those treating chronic health conditions.

3.7.2   The Pre-2012 Dutch Pharmaceutical Pricing Model[5]

Until the end of 2011 the prices of pharmaceuticals and pharmaceutical care in the Netherlands were highly regulated. Dutch pharmacies received an average fee of €7.50 from healthcare insurers for dispensing pharmaceuticals to patients. This fee was set by the Dutch Healthcare Authority. Customized arrangements with insurers for additional services were also permitted, for a maximum fee of €10. The Dutch Pharmaceuticals Pricing Act (Wet Geneesmiddelenprijzen—WGP) determined both the price that manufacturers could ask for their pharmaceuticals (the Taxe) and the Pharmaceuticals Fee System (Geneesmiddelenvergoedings-systeem—GVS), which determined the maximum reimbursement on pharmaceuticals. These amounts, which the Dutch Ministry of Health, Welfare and Sports revised every 6 months, reflected the average price levels for pharmaceuticals in other European countries. While the official list prices for pharmaceuticals mandated by the Dutch government determined the basis on which pharmacies purchased and sold drugs, the difference between official prices and those that pharmacies actually charged to insurers was known as the purchasing margin, which pharmacies received from manufacturers via wholesalers. The 2012 price deregulation eliminated this purchasing margin.

---

[5] This section incorporates data and insights from Mediq (2012).

3.7.3 The 2012 Dutch Pharmaceutical Price Deregulation

In January 2012 the prices for pharmaceuticals and pharmaceutical care were deregulated in the Netherlands. Prices are now based on bilateral agreements between pharmacies and insurers, using the framework defined by the Dutch Healthcare Authority. In addition to dispensing pharmaceuticals, pharmacies advise patients on how to take their medication and on the use of complex pharmaceuticals, ensure patients comply with the therapy, and provide additional medical information to those suffering from chronic illnesses.

In addition, the purchasing of biopharmaceuticals for conditions such as rheumatoid arthritis was transferred to hospital budgets. Previously the cost was covered through basic individual insurance reimbursements. Since Mediq had been accustomed to delivering a substantial amount of these drugs to patients' homes, it began cooperating with hospitals on a fee-for-service basis to continue serving patients and helping them avoid unnecessary hospitalizations.

3.7.4 Mediq's Business Model Transformed

Similarly to other suppliers, prior to 2012 Mediq's revenues came from the fees it earned on the pharmaceuticals it sold. The 2012 deregulation brought an immediate 90 % drop in this type of revenue so the company had to rethink its business model. These developments indicated a clear strategic imperative for Mediq to focus on outcome-based payments.[6]

Mediq's management team recognized the market opportunity of switching from just packaging and distributing medicines and medical supplies to directly catering to the needs of patients. A new integrated pharmaceutical care (IPC) business model with new key value drivers had emerged based on the tangible added value of knowledge-based services and compensation focused on providing patient care. What became important to Mediq was improving the quality of life of patients and preventing avoidable hospitalizations by knowing its customers and tracking their medical treatments.

Having estimated the number of annual hospital admissions that could have been avoided with correct drug use and the total cost that this represented for insurance companies, Mediq developed a proposal that would allow health insurance companies to dramatically reduce costs. It demonstrated and quantified those potential savings and proposed to share the benefits 50:50 with insurers. It started by negotiating a new reimbursement scheme with the largest insurer, Achmea, based on improving adherence (using the drug at the right time); providing the cheapest drug possible; and establishing good communications with "first-line" care providers such as GPs to reduce prescription errors and make further drug recommendations to reduce side-effects.

---

[6] Information provided directly by Mediq.

Since the new reimbursement system did not cover the cost of logistical activities, these were further optimized. Patients could order their repeat prescriptions online, and these were prepared in a central warehouse and delivered to a specified pharmacy for the client to collect. This contributed significantly to reducing errors and inventory levels. The data system also allowed the date and quantity of repeat purchases to be compared with the prescription, and in case of discrepancies, Mediq proactively advised patients on how to improve adherence to their prescribed therapies.

Mediq had thus evolved from having a single traditional profit formula whereby it made its money from the fee collected on the medicines it sold, to having two new and distinct profit formulas that could appear to be contradictory. The first one was based on the margin the company earned on sales of medicines. In this case, the more medicines Mediq sold, the greater its earnings. The second profit formula was based on the savings achieved by keeping its clients healthy. But Mediq's focus was to care for its patients and it thus fostered the second formula, which represented 50 % of the company's total income. From a financial perspective, the two formulas were well balanced and enabled the company to grow.

3.7.5 Mediq's Triple Value Patient-Centric Concept

According to Anco van Marle, Mediq's director of pharmacies and commercial business, the company's core triple-value concept encompassed improved healthcare, increased efficiency and lowered cost (Fig. 3.3).

Mediq's model helped address the issue of how the first link in the pharmaceutical value chain (i.e., a GP or pharmacist) could help reduce costs in the second link

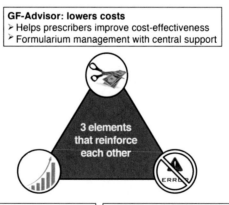

Fig. 3.3 Mediq's IPC lowers costs, increases efficiency and prevents incorrect use of medication (Mediq 2015)

by preventing unnecessary hospitalizations. This concept, which was developed with healthcare insurance companies, included opt-in systems that allowed patients to choose whether to make data available to other parties in the value chain.

Mediq used the customer data that it collected to provide patients with more accurate information about their medical treatments and inform doctors about complementary products to prescribe alongside the main drug to reduce side effects. Examples of such products included a gastric protective agent to prevent stomach ulcers when taking anti-inflammatories, or bisphosphonate for someone with osteoporosis to prevent other potential harmful side effects. Mediq's new business model effectively reduced the number of patients in need of hospitalization due to the inappropriate use of medications, which resulted in overall cost reductions for insurers.

Mediq thus transformed the pharmaceutical retailing model. The ecosystem created with the help of big data brought together healthcare providers, suppliers, authorities, patient organizations and insurers to offer the best medical care to patients. In a traditional value chain, information only travelled in one direction, from consumer to provider. But Mediq collected all the information that was generated along the value chain, analyzed it and then sent customized information back to users based on their specific requirements.

3.7.6 Mediq in Action: A Patient Example

Take the example of Linda, a Mediq user who has hypertension for which she must take a pill daily. Mediq knows this and can prepare Linda's repeat prescription in advance. If she does not show up to collect her medication as expected, Mediq would know that something was wrong—i.e., perhaps she forgot to take some or all of her pills, or she forgot to collect the new batch—and Mediq would contact her to check.

Mediq also developed a device that can be loaded with medicines to be taken at regular intervals and which opens automatically at the required time so that the patient can take the pills. If, for example, Linda failed to operate her system, Mediq would know and take action, probably by contacting her or a member of her family to make sure that Linda is healthy and safe. Similarly with prescriptions purchased at the pharmacy, if she bought too much or too little of a particular medication, Mediq could follow up to check that she was not mismanaging the administration of her medication.

If Linda's doctor modified her prescription, Mediq would be able to assess whether the hypertension pill had been forgotten or whether the doctor had changed the treatment and removed it deliberately. In addition, if Mediq detected an error somewhere in Linda's prescription value chain, for example if a required gastric protection agent had been omitted or if there was an error in the preparation of the prescription, Mediq would be able to know this and contact the necessary persons to fix the problem.

3.7.7 Distribution Redesign

With its new business model, Mediq changed its position in the value chain. It was no longer just a distributor, but an integrated healthcare company that looked after its patients and was a part of a big data ominichain. By reaching its patients directly and through the pharmacy or doctor, Mediq reduced intermediaries and played different roles in the value chain (Fig. 3.4).

Mediq knew exactly 80 % of its demand more than a month in advance, because 80 % of prescriptions were repeats for chronic illnesses, and 99 % of its customers always bought their medication from the same pharmacy. This meant that it only needed to forecast the remaining 20 % of future demand that it was not aware of. Consequently, Mediq's distribution business model changed as well. The inventory level in the pharmacies was cut drastically. It only needed to keep a 24-hour inventory in its pharmacies, which drastically cut its warehousing costs.

Mediq was equally innovative in the way it managed value chain delays. Traditionally, product customization was pushed to the end point of the value chain. For example, printer manufacturers created generic products that were modified in the final stages of the value chain, such as adding components such as the plug to adapt the printer to a specific country. Car manufacturers allowed customers to adapt the end product to their taste, for example by selecting the upholstery, electronic devices and so forth, which were added at the end. Mediq reversed this model. Instead of customizing at the end of the value chain, which in this case would be at the pharmacy, it did this at the warehouse. Big data enabled Mediq to acquire and retain rigorous detail on its customers and adapt the final products further up the value chain. Thus, instead of delivering boxes of drugs in

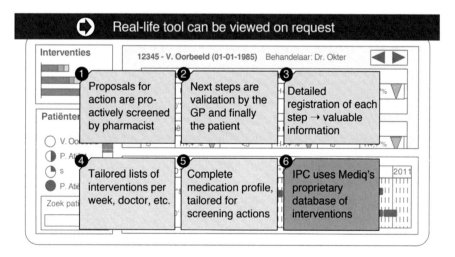

Fig. 3.4 Simplified example of the IPC ICT-system built by Mediq to facilitate a proactive action process (Mediq 2015)

bulk to pharmacies, it delivered small bags containing the prescribed medicines of specific clients. The pharmacy only handled the final sale transaction.

3.7.8 Future Applications

The latest wearable devices are able to capture and share yet more data, and they could make it even easier to monitor medication intake and improve adherence. With this in mind, Mediq's patient-centric model is bound to grow and evolve.

However, while all the participants in the value chain are interested in more data about the market, drug efficacy and patient behaviors in order to improve their performance, the issue of protecting patient privacy has come to the forefront. The lack of clear regulatory guidelines around protecting personalized data has created a bottleneck that is preventing big data from being used to its fullest extent at present.

3.8 Market Opportunity for Big Data in Healthcare in the US[7]

Healthcare is a sizable sector in all developed economies and it is becoming increasingly important in the developing world, too. In the United States, healthcare accounts for slightly more than 17 % of the country's GDP and employs an estimated 11 % of its workforce. Per capita healthcare spending in the United States outpaces that in the countries of the Organisation for Economic Co-operation and Development (OECD) by about 30 %, amounting to $750 billion, or $2500 per person, annually. Over the last decade, US healthcare expenditures have grown by nearly 5 % per year, but despite this increased spending, the United States still underperforms in relation to the OECD average for life expectancy and infant mortality

The ageing US population and the emergence of more expensive health treatments are likely to contribute further to the skyrocketing costs of healthcare. Moreover, operational performance improvements in the US healthcare system have lagged behind other sectors of the economy, making it inefficient and not patient-centric. A reform of the US healthcare system is critical to the US economy and society as a whole. However, the enormous cost and the length of time it takes to implement systemic changes also highlight the importance of finding immediate solutions to improve productivity and decrease costs. Historically, the US healthcare system has not incentivized stakeholders—including doctors, hospitals and other healthcare practitioners—to control costs or optimize efficiency. It has, however, incentivized payments for procedures and medications regardless of their effectiveness or even necessity.

---

[7] This section incorporates data and insights from Manyika et al. (2011).

There are four major pools of data in the US healthcare system:

- provider clinical data
- insurance claims and cost data
- pharmaceutical and medical products R&D data
- patient behavior and sentiment data.

While the amount and quality of available data differs by subsector, digitizing and aggregating clinical data is still in the early stages. An estimated 30 % of it—including medical records, bills, and laboratory and surgery reports—is not being captured electronically. Even when clinical data are available in digital form, they are rarely shared.

The deployment of electronic health records (EHR) by physicians and hospitals was mandated by the American Recovery and Reinvestment Act of 2009, which provided $20 billion in stimulus funding over 5 years to encourage the use of EHRs. This could also be done through outcome-based reimbursement plans, because these would require accurate databases. While insurance companies have long been capturing claims and cost data, the information is not generally in a form that makes it easy to generate real insights because the data sets are fragmented and are often presented in incompatible formats. The pharmaceutical and medical products (PMP) subsector is arguably the most advanced in the United States in terms of digitization and use of healthcare data. Finally, the emerging pool of data related to patient behavior and sentiment could be used to improve adherence to treatment regimens and influence a broad range of lifestyle and wellness activities.

3.9   Value-Based Care

On the path to value-based care, the US Department of Health and Human Services recently mandated that by the end of 2018, 50 % of Medicare payments—equivalent to more than $290 billion per year—would be made through value-based reimbursement models (Porter 2015).

Success and market share growth in the healthcare industry would be driven by the ability of providers to manage the health of the US population in a high-quality and cost-effective way. And profitability would depend on what happens outside hospitals, with remotely enabled patient care. For many healthcare providers, this serves as a strong encouragement for a long-term strategy that they had already chosen to embark upon. In examining the areas comprising the greatest risks and opportunities, post-acute care—which is characterized by highly variable costs and quality of care—comes to the forefront. For example, healthcare providers struggle to monitor outcomes because of limited oversight and control once patients leave the hospital, and the 90-day period after a hospital stay often proves especially challenging.

3.10 Conclusions

Big data presents big opportunities in the pharmaceutical and healthcare industries. The use of big data could help bring about a more effective and efficient system, spur the development of better products and services, and lead to the creation of new patient-centric business models. However, deploying big data requires redesigning the way healthcare has been traditionally provided and funded.

Some countries have made strides to reform their healthcare systems, others are lagging. The example of Mediq and its transformation from a company with the simple task of distributing drugs to a company focused on improving the health of patients is an inspirational story of how big data can help improve outcomes.

References

Cockburn, Robert, Paul N. Newton, E. Kyeremateng Agyarko, Dora Akunyili, Nicholas J White. 2005. The Global Threat of Counterfeit Drugs: Why Industry and Governments Must Communicate the Dangers. Plos Medicine. March 14. http://journals.plos.org/plosmedicine/article?id=10.1371/journal.pmed.0020100. Accessed August 17, 2015.

Cognizant 20–20 Insights. 2013. Pharma serialization: Managing the transformation. January. http://www.cognizant.com/InsightsWhitepapers/Pharma-Serialization-Managing-the-Transformation.pdf. Accessed August 17, 2015.

Deloitte, and Investment Support and Promotion Agency of Turkey (ISPAT). 2014. The pharmaceutical industry in Turkey. March.

Ebel, T., K. George, E. Larsen, K. Shah, and D. Ungerman. 2013. Strategies for creating and capturing value in the emerging ecosystem economy. McKinsey & Company.

Ehrhardt, M., R. Hutchens, and S. Higgins. 2012. Five steps toward a revitalized pharmaceutical supply chain. Strategy + Business, Issue 66, February 28/Spring. http://www.strategy-business.com/article/00094?gko=982c0. Accessed August 17, 2015.

European Commission. 2011. Directive 2011/62/EU of the European Parliament and of the Council. June 8. http://ec.europa.eu/health/files/eudralex/vol-1/dir_2011_62/dir_2011_62_en.pdf. Accessed August 18, 2015.

Healthcare Packaging. 2014. Global Traceability and Serialisation in Pharma. Pharmaceutical Packaging and Labeling Report, 2014. http://www.healthcarepackaging.com/trends-and-issues/traceability-and-authentication/industry-report-global-traceability-and. Accessed August 17, 2015.

Keeling, David, Martin Lösch, and Ulf Schrader. 2010. Outlook on Pharma Operations. McKinsey & Company.

Manufacturing Chemist Pharma. 2013. Joining the dots: A move against counterfeiters. December 9. http://www.manufacturingchemist.com/technical/article_page/Joining_the_dots_a_move_against_counterfeiters/94032. Accessed August 17, 2015.

Frost & Sulivan. 2008. Mass serialisation in the european pharmaceutical industry. Working together on mass serialisation: Whose responsibility is ensuring patient safety? Frost & Sullivan white paper, commissioned by Aegate.

Mediq. 2015. Mediq Pharmacy. Challenges in the Dutch Pharma Market. Company presentation. March 20, 2015.

Mediq. 2012. Annual report 2011. Fees and reimbursements for medical devices and pharmaceuticals. http://annualreport2011.mediq.com/uk/annual_report_2011/system_of_fees_and_reimbursements/. Accessed August 18, 2015.

Manyika, James, Michael Chui, Brad Brown, Jacques Bughin, Richard Dobbs, Charles Roxburgh and Angela Hung Byers. 2011. Big data: The next frontier for innovation, competition, and productivity. McKinsey Global Institute. June.

Porter, B. 2015. Value-based healthcare—Success is no longer about the 1 %. Force Therapeutics, March 18.

Sanofi. 2014. Deployment of serialization in Sanofi Turkey distribution center, business case and return of experience. Company presentation, Geneva, November 5: http://b2b.pharma-iq.com/event.cfm?eventID = 336. Accessed August 18, 2015.

Systech. 2014. Best Practices in Serialization Solution Architecture. Company presentation, Geneva, November 5. http://b2b.pharma-iq.com/event.cfm?eventID = 336. Accessed August 18, 2015.

The Royal Dutch Pharmacists Association (KNMP). 2009. HARM Wrestling. http://www.knmp.nl/search?SearchableText = harm-wrestling. Accessed on August 21, 2015.

World Health Organization. N.d. General information on counterfeit medicines. http://www.who.int/medicines/services/counterfeit/overview/en/. Accessed August 17, 2015.

The Customer Chain: The Omnichannel and the Omnichain

4

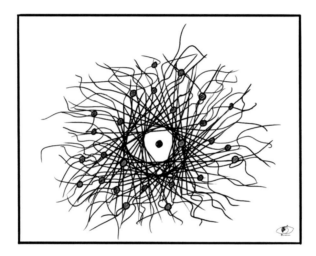

Big data and the digital revolution are rapidly transforming our environment. Consumers are radically changing the way they shop and companies are transforming the way they manage purchasing, sales, transport and logistics operations within their ecosystems as big data allows new ways of communicating within the value chain. Digital trends such as cloud infrastructure, artificial intelligence and the Internet of Things are making it possible for everything to be connected and generate new information. But uncertainty, flexibility and the evolution of economies of scale are also having a strong impact on value chains.

4.1 The Changing Landscape

Big data and the digital revolution are rapidly transforming our environment. Consumers are radically changing the way they shop and companies are transforming the way they manage purchasing, sales, transport and logistics

© Springer International Publishing Switzerland 2016
C. Cordon et al., *Strategy is Digital*, Management for Professionals,
DOI 10.1007/978-3-319-31132-6_4

operations within their ecosystems as big data allows new ways of communicating within the value chain. Digital trends such as cloud infrastructure, artificial intelligence and the Internet of Things are making it possible for everything to be connected and generate new information. But uncertainty, flexibility and the evolution of economies of scale are also having a strong impact on value chains.

These new ways of doing business have only recently become possible and they offer endless prospects. This chapter analyzes their meaning and implications and considers what value chains may look like in a decade or so.

4.1.1   Traditional Versus Current Value Chains

A value chain encompasses all the activities that are needed to deliver a product or service to customers. For example, a traditional value chain for food is from the field to the plate. Value chains used to be quite stable and players had a well-defined role that did not change much. Their behavior was therefore quite predictable unless major unexpected events occurred.

With the advent of big data, hyperconnectivity allows each party within the chain to connect more dynamically with the others, pushing aside rigid models and moving toward a more complex value chain that functions as an ecosystem. In an ecosystem, companies are connected to one another. They occupy a common space in which they can compete and cooperate at the same time. As a result of this permanent contact, their relationships evolve constantly, turning the value chain into a dynamic environment. By definition, value chains generate and process huge amounts of information, which, until recently, technology was not able to handle so the data was often aggregated and the detail was lost. In these circumstances, information might be perceived as excessive or burdensome. Fast-moving consumer goods multinationals, for example, could not treat all the data that retailers generated about their customers, so they tended to condense it to make it easier to manipulate, losing the precious detail in the process. The big data era and substantially improved technological capabilities means that processing and using the vast quantities of information produced at all stages of the value chain is no longer a problem, allowing it to fly fast and accurately in all directions within the ecosystem.

This is not only changing relationships between companies but also making it easier for firms to change roles within the value chain and redefine it almost in real time. Blurring industry boundaries are also making it easier for companies to enter new industries and adopt different positions, something that would have been pretty much unthinkable 30 years ago in view of the extreme rigidness of operating models. A good example of a company that operates in two different industries is Walgreens.

> *Walgreens is a large supermarket chain with in-store drugstores. Over the years, and helped by a number of acquisitions, it has become one of the largest US pharmacy chains (Reuters 2015). More recently it adopted a far more sophisticated offering and modified its role in the value chain. In addition to its in-store pharmacies, which initially just delivered medicines, the company also created health clinics. The combined services of the clinic and the store covered a wide range of services, including issuing prescriptions (so customers no longer have to go to the doctor to obtain a prescription before collecting their medication from the pharmacy) as well as administering vaccinations, performing various health screening tests, treating minor injuries and so forth. Thus, Walgreens, which also maintained its traditional departments (groceries, household goods, etc.), has integrated services that were previously exclusively provided by doctors and/or health clinics, which has allowed it to cover a wider spectrum of the value chain.*
>
> *Big data is one of the elements that allowed Walgreens to do this. In January 2014 the company announced the development of its patient assessment tool and technology platform to support improvements in care across its clinics (MarketWatch 2014). The system brought together insights from more than 8.3 million medical events to the company's health clinic programs, which allowed clinicians to resolve gaps in quality care and "enable ... nurse practitioners and physician assistants to play an increasingly important role as part of a patient's care team" (Peduli 2014).*

4.1.2 The Omnichannel

The emergence of a new consumer with a more proactive approach to purchasing contributed to creating a new landscape characterized by new, non-traditional value chains. As we saw in Chap. 2, car buyers normally go through a five-stage purchasing journey: They start by fantasizing about the possibility of buying a car (stage 1), then decide to do so (stage 2). Next, they evaluate the options (stage 3), shop (stage 4) and finally experience the car and seek external validation (stage 5) (Microsoft 2012). Digital plays an important role in the first three stages as today's consumers gather all the information they need prior to visiting a dealership. Car manufacturers need to adapt by providing these new consumers with the experiences they seek throughout their journey. A distribution channel that has been adapted to these new consumer experiences is called the omnichannel.

The omnichannel combines the use of multiple channels in the shopping experience. Previously, customers would choose one channel and remain in it throughout the whole shopping process. Today all channels are combined and available to consumers, who now have a whole new universe of options at their disposal to customize their personal shopping experience and make it more pleasurable.

Even online shopping has evolved. Whereas the final step was once to have the product delivered to a given address, usually the buyer's home, today multiple delivery options, such as *click and collect* (buy online and collect in the store ... or elsewhere such as a car park, corner shop or 24-h garage for example). Along the same lines, companies that started out as "online marketplaces" are opening physical shops to add the "human touch" to the shopping experience.

In-store shoppers wishing to combine the physical and digital channels can now do so in a variety of ways. According to a Google report, "Consumers still visit stores for more than just transactions, but they now expect more out of any place they shop. They want informed, customized experiences." (Google 2014a).

Many in-store shoppers use their smartphones as an information point, and companies like US beauty and personal care retailer Sephora provide apps for customers to use in their stores to obtain additional information about products on display, inventory and so forth (Google 2014b). But Walgreens has taken the concept of the Omnichannel to a whole new level.

With one in four Americans having access to a Walgreens store within five miles of their home, the company was keen to improve the in-store experience in several ways and encourage customers to buy more. However, while other retailers are trying to figure out how to keep customers in their shops as long as possible, Walgreens is focusing on making the shopping experience more convenient, which also means getting people in and out as fast as possible. It did this by focusing on convenience and customers' needs. Its mobile app allows shoppers to find out information about all kinds of products, from groceries to medicines, and where to locate them in the store so they can find what they need faster. They can save digital discount vouchers or coupons to their reward card, and when their card is scanned at the checkout, the appropriate discounts are automatically deducted. Customers can also opt to receive messages about special offers whenever they enter a Walgreens store, or link their activity tracker to the app to collect points for being active, and then redeem those points against purchases.

Out-of-store app capabilities such as product information, inventories and customizable shopping lists also serve to lure customers into stores, and having a wide mobile presence focuses customers' attention on Walgreens so that they are less inclined to look elsewhere.

A large part of Walgreens' business is related to its in-store pharmacies and health clinics, so its digital strategy also integrates several convenience services such as being able to fill in prescriptions in a couple of taps on the screen of their mobile or setting up an automatic pill reminder. In an effort to further "humanize" the service, a Pharmacy Chat messaging service allows customers to ask a pharmacist questions about their prescription for example, and its "telehealth" platform allows virtual patient visits for those unable to physically get themselves to a healthcare provider (Milnes 2015).

The Walgreens example demonstrates that the combinations of digital tools and options to keep customers interested, bring them into physical stores and ensure the shopping experience is as pleasant and seamless as possible are seemingly endless.

4.1.3 The Market of One: Personalized Marketing in the Omnichannel

Building on the omnichannel, the market of one concept refers to personalized marketing that establishes a one-to-one relationship between the customer and the company and introduces new ways for companies to tailor their approach to each customer. This kind of marketing goes into so much detail in the interaction with clients that it offers real-time information developed specifically for each one. In 2012 US-based online travel agency Orbitz.com experimented with displaying different hotel rates to Mac and PC visitors. By tracking user behavior, Orbitz discovered that Mac users spent on average $20 to $30 more a night on hotels than their PC counterparts (Mattioli 2012).

This practice, which is known as dynamic pricing, allows e-commerce platforms to adapt the price of their products based on market demand and the perception of how much customers are willing to pay for a product (Petro 2015).

However, dynamic pricing can be dangerous when it turns into price discrimination (adapting the price of a single product depending on how rich the country in which the customer lives is). Such instances have been in the news lately. Disneyland Paris allegedly overcharged British and German customers on the basis of where they lived and the European Commission is questioning the legality of this practice (Barker 2015). And Apple's new music service, Apple Music, has been pointed at for its differentiated pricing as it charges customers in India $2 for a one-month personal subscription for which some European customers are charged $14, seven times more, though some European countries (Greece, Portugal) are charged less (Horwitz 2015).

4.2 The Omnichain

Just as marketing and sales are progressing toward the market of one within the omnichannel, value chains are adapting to the new situation and being transformed by the big data revolution as they evolve toward a new scenario in which they re-configure themselves in real time, making it possible to design, produce, plan and deliver products and services almost individually.

The omnichain is an ecosystem in which companies interact and complement each other's capabilities. Just as the omnichannel covers everything from delivery to customer experience, the omnichain encompasses the entire value chain, expanding the same concept of dynamism and flexibility from suppliers to customer experience. In omnichains any player can rapidly change and assume new positions fast. Traditional value chains were designed around physical constraints that assumed limited access to information about products and their location so they had to be planned in a consolidated way, with large-scale production of huge orders irrespective of actual demand because computer power was simply not available and access to data was limited. Now value chains are modular, with elements that can be reconfigured in real time, allowing companies to create their own omnichains by selecting and arranging their preferred modules in the best way to achieve their desired revenue, risk profile or time-to-market objectives. Digitization, vastly improved technology and big data have made it possible for companies to design, produce, plan and deliver products and services at an almost individual level to cater for small orders.

Similarly, technological limitations once meant that companies could only cope with a maximum of four or five value chains at a time because it was too complicated for them to manage more. Today's landscape requires more adaptable value chains to comply more accurately with market demands.

Take smartphones for example. Apple consumers differ from Samsung consumers, who in turn differ from other smartphone users. Apple users might be willing to wait, if necessary, to get the device they want, whereas someone who was originally looking for a particular LG device may opt for a different model or even brand if the initial choice is not available immediately. Phone retailers know this and need to be prepared to cater for different types of customer. They will need to work with different value chains depending on the smartphone model. For iPhones, more stocks will be needed and if retailers run out of devices they need to be able to order additional ones quickly and easily. For other brands, which are more interchangeable, retailers have more flexibility and can offer various alternatives to the final customer based on availability.

Traditionally, companies designed and optimized different value chains to fulfill consumer demands based on sales forecasts. This involved stocking large quantities of products in warehouses, irrespective of lifecycle expectations or risks from currency fluctuations, products becoming obsolete, pressure from competition, etc.). Today, companies are moving toward a more granular segmentation with well-differentiated operating models by segment. This segmentation is being managed more dynamically. Digital capabilities should enable real-time operating model configuration including trading partners, assets, processes, organization and governance.

The omnichain affects every stage of the value chain:

- **Design** Product design and development is no longer restricted to in-company experts. Consumers now have the opportunity to play an active role by suggesting modifications to an existing product, and these changes can be implemented speedily. Similarly, the amount of connections that the value chain creates and the way information can now be shared makes it possible for multiple companies to collaborate on the same design.
- **Making** Methods such as 3D printing or digital manufacturing have made it possible for a factory to receive instructions digitally and adapt the production line automatically. As a consequence, the company can make a brand new item

in a short time, shortcutting previous steps and sending the order directly to manufacturing rather than involving every supply chain level as was the case before.

- **Buying** Transparency increases and information about suppliers, prices, contracts and conditions is updated in real time and through multiple channels. Information can therefore be compared much faster and more options are available.
- **Moving** The availability of real-time information increases supply chain efficiency and speed, thus preventing bottlenecks.
- **Planning** The huge amount of information provided by the value chain makes it easier for different players to make faster and more automated decisions. This is key because it implies that some steps previously requiring human intervention can now be automated. In addition, it helps anticipate the whole system's future behavior.
- **Service** The relationship with the consumer becomes more complex as products evolve from what they used to be, just devices, to an experience. Many B2B companies have switched from selling physical products to offering complete services or solutions related to the original products. For example Michelin used to just sell tires, now it offers a range of related services such as the Michelin Fleet Solutions with a customized tire leasing program.
- **Product** Products are now enhanced with additional digital components and other customized services that allow consumers to interact a lot more, which changes the whole consumer experience from linear and one-directional to non-linear and interactive.

The omnichain is iterative. In traditional value chains information flow was linear, from the client to the distributor to the manufacturer. Today's value chains are more like neurons, constantly developing new connections throughout the ecosystem. All players are information senders and receivers generating multiple flows and multidirectional exchanges of information. In this new multidimensional universe the information travels in all directions.

4.2.1 An Example from the Pharmaceutical Industry

Chapter 3 describes extensively how major Dutch healthcare company Mediq is transforming the way healthcare has been traditionally understood. Its ecosystem brings together healthcare providers, suppliers, professionals, authorities, patient organizations and insurers to offer its customers the best medical care. Figure 4.1 compares a traditional value chain with Mediq's current ecosystem.

Other industry players are following suit, moving toward ecosystems in which information travels in many directions. In a traditional value chain the information would only travel from the consumer, backward to the professionals and providers. Now pharmaceutical companies collect information generated throughout the value chain, analyze it, then send back new, customized information to final users based

Fig. 4.1 Traditional value chain versus Mediq's ecosystem

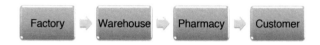

Traditional value chain

Mediq's ecosystem

on their specific needs. Take the case of Linda, for example, who has hypertension and needs to take a pill daily. The healthcare company knows this and can prepare in advance the medication that she will need to buy the following month at the pharmacy. If Linda does not pick up the medication as expected, the healthcare company will know that something is wrong (for example, it may be that she forgot to either take pills or to buy them) and will contact her to follow up. If Linda's doctor modified her prescriptions, thanks to the big data information collected by Mediq, the healthcare company will be able to assess whether the doctor forgot to include the hypertension pills or if he changed the treatment and removed it deliberately.

These value chains are evolving from a wholesaler to a big data omnichain. In the case of Mediq, even its mission has changed (see Chap. 3) from distributor to healthcare company that looks after its patients. By reaching them directly and through the pharmacy or doctor, it has reduced the number of intermediaries and is playing different roles in the value chain. Mediq knows what 80 % of its demand will be more than a month in advance, because 80 % of prescriptions are repeats for chronic illnesses, and 99 % of customers always buy in the same pharmacy, so the company pretty much only needs to apply predictive forecasting to the remaining 20 % of its demand. This has had a major impact on Mediq's distribution channel because by knowing what 80 % of its demand will be, it only needs to keep a 24-hour inventory in its warehouses, thereby massively reducing stocks.

The pharma industry is also innovating in the way it handles value chain postponement, which consists in pushing product customization to the end of the value chain. Printer manufacturers for example, created generic products that were adapted in the final stages of the value chain, for example by adding a plug or converter to adapt the printer to a specific country. Some pharma companies have now reversed this strategy and instead of customizing at the end of the value chain, i.e., at the pharmacy, they do so at the warehouse and then distribute the customized final product to the pharmacies to be sold to the final customers.

4.3 Drivers and Dilemmas of the Evolution Toward the Omnichain

The emergence of the omnichain is the consequence of several drivers that are reshaping the way ecosystems function. This evolution brings its own difficulties. Moving toward the omnichain implies dealing with dilemmas that have co-existed for years in value chains and which remain relevant, and companies will increasingly find themselves having to make decisions based on their specific circumstances. There is no right or wrong option, no one-size-fits-all solution.

4.3.1 Key Drivers

There are several drivers behind the evolution of value chains toward the omnichain as described below.

Uncertainty An essential aspect of managing value chains effectively at all stages (supply, distribution, etc.) was being able to handle uncertainty. Big data provides a lot more information about demand. Logically this should reduce uncertainty. But customers have also become more volatile as a result of having more information at their disposal, so they react faster to the market, which again adds uncertainty to the process.

Flexibility Value chains need to be more flexible to be able to handle this increasing uncertainty. Big data helps all players in the value chain react faster, because today it is possible to know what is happening throughout the value chain in real time. For example, a village retailer awaiting supplies may barely notice a slight delay in the delivery of his order due to a problem in the production line that has required stopping and re-planning. Three decades ago, the retailer might have waited for days for information about why his goods had not arrived. Today, he would probably not even know something had gone wrong because as soon as a production line breaks down, the supply chain tower is notified, potential solutions are analyzed in real time, the optimum one is selected and everything goes back to normal in no time, avoiding a blockage in the value chain. Traditional value chains were too slow and rigid and could not react with today's flexibility and agility.

Economies of Scale It is not new that the more units of a product a company produces, the cheaper the cost per unit. Nothing has changed there. But big data has reduced the minimum scale. For example, some years ago, if you needed business cards you had to order at least 1000 because it was so expensive to produce the initial plate. With digital printing, no plate is required and you can print as many or as few as you want because the initial investment for the layout is minimal. The market of one whereby products are personalized to individuals is also reshaping economies of scale.

4.3.2   Open Dilemmas

The arrival of the omnichain and all the changes in the ecosystem are aggravating at least two dilemmas that have co-existed for years with value chains. These dilemmas need to be reconsidered and reevaluated.

Uncertainty Versus Risk Minimization This is one of the main dilemmas that constantly comes up. Companies complain that their forecasting is never good enough. One of the strategies for managing uncertainty is to play with the stock. If the forecast is not well done or accurate enough (i.e., it has a high error margin), the company's stocks need to cover what the forecast is not able to predict. The omnichain can minimize the risk of running out of stock but it can also react swiftly if it does run out. One of Mediq's dilemmas, for example, was the quantity of products that manufacturers, distributors and pharmacies should stock. Previously it would have had to have months-worth of supplies in stock. Now it only needs a day's worth because it knows what 80 % of its total demand is, which dramatically minimizes its risk. The uncertainty has practically disappeared. However, with the new technologies came a new kind of customer that has increased volatility in the demand of certain products, which is increasing uncertainty at that end.

Flexibility Versus Economies of Scale Value chains have evolved to become much more flexible and can be handled almost individually. Whereas previously a company could not handle more than five or six value chains at a time, the omnichain allows granularity to such an extent that it could be hard to know when to stop. There was a time when pharmacies made preparations onsite and on demand, but this service had disappeared because of the cost and complexity.

Today it is once again a reality, except that instead of remedies being prepared at the drugstore, they are being produced at distribution centers, which are equipped with the necessary machines, resources and chemical compounds.

An agile and flexible value chain cannot achieve economies of scale, and an efficient value chain with economies of scale cannot be fast and flexible. Faster, however, is not always better. It is in the best interests of companies to determine their optimal speed and manage it proactively, finding the right granularity of the value chain for best results. Inditex, the world's biggest apparel company, has a faster and more flexible value chain than its competitors, which allows the company to better manage risks and seize opportunities by adapting to short-term consumer trends. Inditex is credited with creating a new business model, fast-fashion, in which a fast value chain is the critical element for success. However, for big multinationals, faster does not mean *as fast as they could*. Inditex found the right balance to beat competitors and offer high flexibility by preserving economies of scale that allow it to keep product prices low while ensuring the company is profitable and successful (Cordón and Ferreiro 2014).

4.4 The Impact of Big Data on the Value Chain

The broad adoption of digital in value chains is bringing with it changes to their traditional landscape. Industry boundaries are blurring, opening up new prospects for companies to compete with other organizations that would have been out of their scope previously. Big data also implies that everything is connected, creating fresh ways to communicate within the value chain and new information senders. Other digital trends such as cloud infrastructure or artificial intelligence are also having a strong impact on value chains.

4.4.1 Frenemies with Everybody: Minecraft, LEGO and Microsoft

When all players can play all cards, collaborating and competing at the same time, everybody becomes a frenemy (friend + enemy) with everybody. Sectors are no longer rigid and well defined so companies can jump freely from one to another. A good example of a situation in which players that, 20 years ago, would never have been competitors, is one involving LEGO, Minecraft and Microsoft. In September 2014 Microsoft acquired Mojang, the company that made Minecraft—a video game that was created by a Swedish programmer almost for fun and that became one of the best-selling video games of all times. The objective of the game was to build worlds in a given space using a set of tools that were either provided at the beginning of the game or collected by users as they played. This was similar to a LEGO game, except that Minecraft was digital and LEGO was physical. Minecraft became what LEGO called a "frenemy"—an enemy, because the game objectives were the same and therefore so were the potential customers, and a friend because they formed a partnership whereby LEGO created the physical Minecraft tools and bricks. Meanwhile, when Microsoft entered the playing field by acquiring Mojang, it became a competitor of LEGO, which would have been unthinkable before the development of digital games.

On June 1, 2015, months after Microsoft acquired Minecraft, the relationship between LEGO and Minecraft became more competitive than friendly when LEGO released LEGO Worlds, a new sandbox video game that experts say takes the block-building experience way further than Mojang's version (Robertson 2015).

4.4.2 The Internet of Things

Big data encompasses many things, from 3D printing to data generated by users through social networks. Another important chunk of big data is also generated by devices. This is called the Internet of Things (or IoT), and its impact on the value chain is growing rapidly.

The IoT is the "networked connection of physical objects" (DHL 2015), which means that Internet connections are now extended to physical objects that can virtually talk among themselves and interact with humans. It is as if every single device had an integrated smartphone and could send and receive information through the Internet. The flow of information generated by these connections has a tremendous impact on the omnichain because it makes it possible to monitor the entire value chain and every product at any stage, which helps improve the whole chain. It is bidirectional in that not only do devices provide information but also instructions can be sent to devices to modify their behavior. The fact that all players, all devices and all steps are interconnected creates new information flows that once again help configure and reconfigure the value chain.

> *Since 2013 Zara has been using radio frequency identification (RFID), a technology that has existed for more than 10 years, to track all its products (Bjork 2014). Each garment is identified individually with a chip that allows real-time knowledge about where every item is throughout the entire distribution-to-sale process. This represents a revolution in value chain management, because it allows, among other things, much more accurate stock management and a better in-store customer service. Customers can ask about a product and a size and obtain real-time information about its availability and the possibility of having it delivered from a store or from zara.com (Inditex n.d.). With the implementation of RFID, Zara has shown how the IoT is impacting the value chain as well as people's lives.*

The IoT also relates to wearables—miniature electronic devices worn by users—and the data they generate. For example activity trackers such as FitBit, Google Glass or iWatch measure and record the distance and pace of an activity such as walking or running. Companies are using these in different ways. Healthcare companies are working on devices to help patients track specific health issues. Google and Novartis, for example, are developing smart contact lenses that could measure glucose in tear fluid and send the data wirelessly to a mobile device. The technology could be life-changing for many diabetics who, at present, have to check their blood sugar levels by pricking their finger and analyzing a drop of blood, sometimes as often as 10 times a day (Copley 2014). Google also plans to use these contact lenses and other tools in its Baseline Study, a project that will collect anonymous genetic and molecular information from 175 people—and later thousands more—to map what a healthy human should look like. It is hoped that it will be possible one day to detect health risks such as heart disease or cancer at an early stage and take preventative action where possible (Levy 2014).

The IoT is not the future, it is the present. In many cases, it does not involve leading-edge technological innovations, but rather implementing existing technology to extend value chain capabilities. In fact, RFIDs and other kinds of sensors to measure, for example, temperature, pressure, presence or light have existed for many years. It is the ability to cope with the massive volumes of data generated by the widespread application of these devices that has turned the IoT into a buzzword.

4.4.3 Big Data and the Digital Revolution

According to Wikipedia, "big data is a broad term for data sets so large or complex that traditional data processing applications are inadequate. Challenges include analysis, capture, data curation, search, sharing, storage, transfer, visualization, and information privacy." The value chain is being profoundly transformed by the digital revolution. Big data is one of its most important elements but it is not the only one. Other digital trends strongly contributing to that transformation are:

- **Cloud infrastructures**: Beyond increasing storage capacity and reducing infrastructure costs, clouds allow real-time information exchange.
- **Internet of Things**: Big data captured via the IoT can be applied to implement instructions that modify the behavior of the different elements as needed.
- **Artificial intelligence:** This allows autonomous decision-making processes that enable faster reaction to events.

One development that was fundamental in leading us to this digital evolution is the huge increase in data storage capacity over the last few decades.

In the 1960s Material Requirements Planning (MRP) was developed to help companies plan their manufacturing activities. Companies used a computer program to list the materials they needed to purchase in order to manufacture their goods.

The next step, manufacturing resource planning (MRP II), added the possibility of checking the company's resources, including labor, machine capacity and materials. The goal was to provide consistent data to all players in the manufacturing process as the product moved through the production line.

Distribution resource planning (DRP) went a step further by focusing on distribution instead of manufacturing. This involved asking retailers what they needed so that manufacturers could adjust their production, inventory and stocks more accurately.

These three models were created to cover the needs of companies at the time. Gradually, software companies developed complex programs that facilitated what had turned into a difficult planning exercise involving huge amounts of information. Computer capacity was limited, however, which restricted the possibilities. Companies tended to aggregate information from their retailers instead of preserving its granularity because their systems could not handle the detail.

There were also other problems that required workarounds. For example, processes had to be sequenced because it was not possible to optimize the entire problem at once; sub-optimizations had to be made for the different echelons of the chain; and decisions had to be planned synchronously in agreed time buckets, typically weekly or monthly.

Data capture and computing time did not allow for re-planning exceptions during execution. We saw in the example used to describe flexibility that a village retailer awaiting supplies today may barely notice a slight delay in the delivery of his order due to a problem in the production line, whereas three decades ago he might have waited for days for information about why his goods had not arrived. When a disruption affected the chain, computers were not capable of integrating a fresh information update and re-computing, so the value chain and its decision-making process had to be fragmented, creating two different worlds: planning and execution.

These problems are no longer an issue, and companies like Mediq are reinterpreting the models. Instead of aggregating information about demand obtained from pharmacies, which would mean losing information about the individuals, the big data revolution is making it possible for them to use the detail to customize their final products at their warehouses. Thus, when they distribute products to pharmacies, instead of delivering a box with 100 packages of medicine A and 200 packages of medicine B, for example, they can deliver small bags containing the individual prescriptions for customer X, Y or Z. Pharmacies only sell the final product to the consumer.

Mediq's omnichain example prompts us to explore new possibilities and new models to drive and structure our companies, because the previous ones no longer fulfill today's complex needs.

In the coming years, new models will be able to handle all the information that we store now; some of that information comes from the development of the IoT and its impact on the value chain. In fact, big data is creating the biggest revolution in value chains in the last 50 years, even more so than when the first computers were introduced and made it possible to eliminate warehouses and intermediaries all over the world. Today's digital revolution is allowing value chains to operate in dramatically different ways:

- Instead of having to plan decisions synchronously within an agreed time frame, value chains can be adapted in real-time to meet changing customer needs.
- Today's value chains allow end-to-end optimization, which means that they look and extend beyond the boundaries of the organization to the whole ecosystem.
- Value chains are now characterized by their granularity in that they can plan and operate at the most detailed level, i.e., individual products, consumers or events.
- They have been automated, displacing the role of humans to the most sophisticated and complex activities.

Where companies once accepted that there were aspects they did not and could not know and that the information they had had to be aggregated because computers could not cope with the large amount of data, today's big data transformation has blown these problems out of the window as it has eliminated uncertainty and dramatically changed the concepts of both economies of scale and flexibility.

Many companies have found it difficult to forecast what, when and how consumers will buy. Big data is changing the way they do their forecasting. Rather than using a sample of past demand to forecast future sales, some companies are predicting the behavior of individuals based on their actions. One example is Amazon's *anticipatory shipping* whereby it sends items closer to final customers before the transaction has been made, in the hope (based on the data that the company has analyzed) that the customer will soon complete the process.

A real example of anticipatory shipping is that of an Amazon user in Sweden who ordered a bike through the website. The bike was supposed to be shipped from the United States, so the user was expecting around two to three weeks of delivery time. Amazingly, she received it one day later. How did this happen? Amazon had tracked this user's visits to its website and analyzed her behavior. She had already clicked on the item several times in different sessions, so many times that Amazon concluded that eventually, she would buy the bicycle. Forecasting a future behavior based on assumptions emerging from the data analysis, Amazon shipped the bicycle before it was even bought. The company claims that it is continuously working to improve the consumer experience. This is good proof of it.

4.5   Is the Future Evolutive or Disruptive?

We saw earlier that uncertainty, flexibility and economies of scale are some of the main drivers leading us to the omnichain. We have also seen how companies need to adapt to this new environment by diversifying their products and being open to explore new industry sectors with new competitors and new frenemies. That is our present reality. But to what extent will the omnichain affect companies, markets and consumers in the future? We have imagined two different scenarios that may reflect what value chains will look like and how they will behave in 10 years' time.

4.5.1   Evolutive-2001: A Space Odyssey

Looking back we see that the development of systems and applications to help companies manage their value chains started in the 1960s with MRP. Gradually, companies grew more complex and so did their systems.

The new millennium marked a transition period for IT. Big corporations were spending huge amounts of money to migrate their data to SAP and other large platforms. The hefty IT budgets led them to question the true competitive advantage of customization over standardization of what was gradually being perceived as a commodity.

Oracle, the giant software company created in the late 1970s, has maintained its leading position as a business applications provider. With the new millennium, Oracle changed its strategy to transform from being a best-of-breed, dominant niche player to becoming a strategic partner for global organizations, delivering more value and enabling them to develop a global infrastructure strategy. A period of acquisitions started and culminated with the rollout of Oracle "Red Stack," a new vision in business IT that offered an integrated package including servers, storage, operating systems, applications, etc. (Cordón 2012).

This evolution was pushed by market needs. Software companies like Oracle worked on the basis of what organizations lacked to improve their functioning.

New theoretical models will appear, building on the current ones to help us manage the big data landscape. Their starting point will probably be today's huge amount of information and the granularity of value chains. The theoretical frameworks will be followed by new IT developments. It will be a slow and progressive evolution characterized by the emergence of new models that will build on what we have.

This future is similar to what the movie *2001: A Space Odyssey* portrays: a slow, tidy and centralized world resulting from a predictable step-by-step evolution.

4.5.2   Disruptive: Blade Runner

In total opposition to an evolutive future is the blade runner one where companies realize that the models they are currently using to manage their business are no longer valid because they cannot handle the data and granularity of today's reality. New competitors will emerge with business models designed around value generated from big data. These models will offer solutions to the latest problems. This future would imply a fast change in the way we function. Flexe is one company that could illustrate this.

Flexe is a marketplace for warehouse space. It offers on-demand warehousing, connecting organizations in need of additional space with organizations with extra space. Rather than following the path of what already existed in the warehousing industry before them and improving current systems, Flexe created a new concept and a new business model from scratch using big data as its foundation. If after five or six years the industry sector realizes that Flexe works better than the traditional models, the new disruptive scenario will take over and warehousing as it has been understood up until now will disappear.

The blade runner future would be characterized by fast changes that instead of requiring new models, could develop independent routines that help companies make decisions organically, in real time. Just as airlines change their offering in real time, what if traditional companies like LEGO or Nike were to do the same thing and adapt in real time the products they are manufacturing based on demand?

As in the movie *Blade Runner*, this future proposes an integrated chaos that works rapidly and efficiently.

4.6 Conclusions

With the advent of big data, value chains have evolved into complex networks in which all players are connected to one-another, competing and collaborating at the same time.

Consumers are radically changing the way they shop, using multiple channels to find out more information before deciding what product they want and where to buy it. Companies need to adapt their marketing and sales operations to this new consumer experience, develop new strategies to communicate and engage with their consumers, and offer a consistent message across all channels. This is the omnichannel.

Big data and the digital revolution are not only affecting marketing and sales. They are also rapidly transforming entire value chains into flexible, modular and reconfigurable omnichains. The omnichain is an ecosystem that turns the existing linear supply chain into a multidimensional system that stretches in all directions, creating new connections all the time, like neurons. The omnichain can manage different types of demands by being able to identify every single piece or component with its location and handle it in a differentiated way. Even consumers can step in and share their feedback at any time during production, instead of just with the retailer after delivery of the final product. In the past, each customer segment had specific needs, which required a different supply chain in each case. Today, this distinction has disappeared and a single, multitiered supply chain is able to manage all the different customer segments as any player can change and assume new positions fast.

Big data and the digital revolution are also affecting the traditional industry landscape. Companies can enter new industry sectors by competing and collaborating simultaneously with their frenemies, blurring industry boundaries in the process.

Companies will have to anticipate and adapt to these changes. We imagined two different futures that could become real within a decade: The evolutive future, which we called 2001: A space odyssey, and the disruptive future, which we called blade runner.

We believe that the blade runner future is more likely to happen because big data and the IoT are dismantling some of the constraints that we have been facing for the last 40 years. The new situation can open up many possibilities for creating novel and more cost-effective business models.

Take Xiaomi—the manufacturer of low-cost smartphones, mobile apps and other consumer electronics—which sold over two million phones in a 12-hour online sale (Low 2015). This points to a new way of doing business that has only recently become possible. Previously, the inability of computers to handle huge amounts of information would have made such an online sale impossible. As these difficulties are swept aside, the prospects are endless.

References

Barker, Alex. 2015. High Ho! Disneyland Paris faces Brussels pricing probe. FT.com. July 28. http://www.ft.com/intl/cms/s/0/27e42c8e-351d-11e5-b05b-b01debd57852. html#axzz3iUJJdOSG. Accessed August 13, 2015.

Bjork, Christopher. 2014. Zara builds its business around RFID. Wall Street Journal. September 16. http://www.wsj.com/articles/at-zara-fast-fashion-meets-smarter-inventory-1410884519? mod=dist_smartbrief. Accessed August 10, 2015.

Copley, Caroline. 2014. Google found a partner to make its futuristic contact lenses. BusinessInsider. July 15. http://www.businessinsider.com/google-found-a-partner-to-make-its-futuristic-contact-lenses-2014-7#ixzz3d8UKVqDM. Accessed August 10, 2015.

Cordón, Carlos, and Teresa Ferreiro. 2014. The Value Chain Shift: Seven Future Challenges Facing Top Executives, Chapter 6. Lausanne, Switzerland: IMD, IMD Global Value Chain Center.

Cordón, Carlos, Fang Liu, Philippe Margery, and Ralf Seifert. 2012. Oracle: An evolution of the IT paradigm. IMD case study no. IMD-6-0336.

DHL. 2015. Internet of Things in logistics. DHL Trend Research, Cisco Consulting Services. http://www.dhl.com/content/dam/Local_Images/g0/New_aboutus/innovation/ DHLTrendReport_Internet_of_things.pdf. Accessed August 10, 2015.

Google. 2014a. Digital impact on in-store shopping: Research debunks common myths. October. https://think.storage.googleapis.com/docs/digital-impact-on-in-store-shopping_research-stud ies.pdf. Accessed August 10, 2015.

Google. 2014b. New research shows how digital connects shoppers to local stores. October. https://www.thinkwithgoogle.com/articles/how-digital-connects-shoppers-to-local-stores. html. Accessed August 10, 2015.

Horwitz, Josh. 2015. Apple Music is just $2 in India—80% cheaper than the US. Quartz. July 1. http://qz.com/442296/apple-music-is-just-2-per-month-in-india-80-cheaper-than-the-us/. Accessed August 13, 2015.

Inditex. N.d. Radio Frequency Identification (RFID) Project. https://www.inditex.com/documents/10279/32381/RFID_eng_low.pdf/79ae6492-752c-4f51-803b-ddb0de92d7cb. Accessed August 10, 2015.

Levy, Karyne. 2014. Google is going to collect information to try and figure out the perfectly healthy human. BusinessInsider. July 24. http://www.businessinsider.com/google-baseline-study-2014-7#ixzz3d8VpIrzf. Accessed August 10, 2015.

Low, Aloysius. 2015. Xiaomi sells over 2 million phones in 12-hour online sale. CNET, April, 8. http://www.cnet.com/news/xiaomi-mi-fan-festival-ends-with-a-bang-with-over-2-million-phones-sold/. Accessed August 10, 2015.

MarketWatch. 2014. Walgreens Brings Big Data Analytics to Healthcare Clinics Through Expanded Relationship with Inovalon. January 30. http://www.marketwatch.com/story/walgreens-brings-big-data-analytics-to-healthcare-clinics-through-expanded-relationship-with-inovalon-2014-01-30. Accessed August 10, 2015.

Mattioli, Dana. 2012. On Orbitz, Mac users steered to pricier hotels. Wall Street Journal, August 23. http://www.wsj.com/articles/SB10001424052702304458604577488822667325882. Accessed August 10, 2015.

Microsoft. 2012. The Consumer Journey: Global Auto-Buyers. Report based on research conducted by Ipsos Media CT and Ipsos OTX, commissioned by Microsoft, February–June 2012.

Milnes, Hilary. 2015. Walgreens uses mobile apps to solve in-store headaches. Digiday. May 4. http://digiday.com/brands/walgreens-uses-mobile-apps-solve-store-headaches/. Accessed August 13, 2015.

Pedulli, Laura. 2014. Walgreens turns to big data analytics to improve care. Clinical Innovation and Technology. Feb 3. http://www.clinical-innovation.com/topics/analytics-quality/walgreens-turns-big-data-analytics-improve-care. Accessed August 10, 2015.

Petro, Greg. 2015. Dynamic pricing: Which customers are worth the most? Amazon, Delta Airlines and Staples weigh in. Forbes. April 17. http://www.forbes.com/sites/gregpetro/2015/04/17/dynamic-pricing-which-customers-are-worth-the-most-amazon-delta-airlines-and-staples-weigh-in/1/. Accessed August 10, 2015.

Reuters. 2015. Walgreens December same-store sales beat estimates. Jan 6. http://www.reuters.com/article/2015/01/06/walgreen-results-idUSL3N0UL4XF20150106. Accessed August 10, 2015.

Robertson, Andy. 2015. "LEGO Worlds" expands beyond "Minecraft" horizons. June 8. Forbes. http://www.forbes.com/sites/andyrobertson/2015/06/08/lego-worlds-minecraft-review/. Accessed August 10, 2015.

Bikes or Drones to the Consumer: The Logistical Challenge of the Last Mile

5

This chapter delves into the logistics and transportation section of the value chain and analyzes the challenges and opportunities arising from the massive rise in the volume of e-commerce. We use examples of traditional players like Yamato Logistics, which is relying on big data to survive, as well as new players from other industries, like Uber and Amazon, which are leveraging their big data know-how to enter an industry that, up until now, was only accessible to a few.

5.1 Changes in the Logistics Industry

The transport and logistics industry is experiencing a complete regeneration due to the changes and innovations brought about by big data, such as the Internet of Things (IoT) and the evolution of e-commerce. Uber—a transportation network

© Springer International Publishing Switzerland 2016
C. Cordon et al., *Strategy is Digital*, Management for Professionals,
DOI 10.1007/978-3-319-31132-6_5

company worth $50 billion known for its app aimed at connecting people seeking transportation with drivers using their private cars—is experimenting with other ideas, including parcel deliveries (Macmillan 2015). At the time of writing, this initiative was not working as hoped.

Traditionally, the most expensive and complicated part of delivering goods has always been the "last mile," the final leg of the journey between the hub and the ultimate destination. The reason it is so expensive is that it is individualized, i.e., one person has to physically take each parcel to its final destination whereas the first part of the journey up to the delivery hub is shared with many other parcels. A delivery company in a city like New York, for example, would ideally want to be able to group as many packages as possible for distribution to a particular address (the last mile), because the effort of loading the truck with parcels and delivering them is pretty much the same for one or 20 parcels. But if the company delivers 20 packages to the same address, it is paid 20 times for a service that it would have to perform anyway for a single parcel. This is another example of the economies of scale discussed in Chap. 4.

Big data makes it possible to track packages in real time. This allows logistics companies to know where their packages are at any given moment, including when they are on the move. They can also know which routes are most and least popular, which are the slowest and fastest and so forth. Big data is vital to controlling these factors and improving efficiency.

The development of e-commerce has, for its part, generated a massive increase in the number of package consignments. This has, in turn, created a new market in an industry where various types of customers have additional needs. As explained in Chap. 2, buyers use many channels to make their purchases and they expect a variety of delivery options (in the shop, at home or at some other pickup point). Every day, e-commerce engenders millions of transactions that translate into parcels to be delivered. The omnichain (discussed in detail in Chap. 4) has evolved to such an extent that the whole process has changed and the entire value chain is going through a deep transformation right at its core.

It is also, in turn, reshaping industries and businesses. The value chain has gained in relevance compared to the early days when it played a minor role in companies' strategies. In many ways it is at the heart of the big data revolution. But the evolution toward the omnichain is now reshaping the essence of companies. For example, some companies, like Amazon, are transforming and reinventing themselves every day, anticipating customer behaviors and shipping products before purchases have been made based on information provided by big data.

This chapter analyzes the impact of the changing landscape on the logistics industry using the example of Yamato—Japan's largest door-to-door delivery service with a market share of 42 % (Morgan 2014)—to understand the way big data is affecting this sector. We also look at other innovative companies to illustrate the possible futures that we believe are to come. In other chapters we used real successful examples of what is already happening to illustrate the impact of big data. In the case of the logistics industry, our research reveals that many players are still working on their shift toward big data and have not yet gone through the deep transmutation that we expect will happen in the coming years. They have nevertheless come a long way in improving their processes and maximizing their effectiveness, and in so doing they are reinventing how they manage their business.

5.2   Yamato: The Traditional Logistics Industry

Japan has always been an insular country, both at a business and a social level, particularly since the seventeenth century when it closed off its borders to all but a couple of countries for fear of invasion. Its borders remained closed to the Western world until the signing of the Treaty of Kanagawa in 1854, which opened Japanese ports to US merchant ships and marked the end of Japan's seclusion. At the time, Japan was 40–60 years behind Western countries in terms of development. In the West, people and goods were already being transported by rail but the Japanese were still using donkeys as their principle means of transport. When Japan finally opened up to the rest of the world, this lag fostered Japan's high-speed journey toward industrialization, and before long the country had become a global player and industry leader in many areas, including transportation and technology.

It is in this context that in 1919 a small transport company called Yamato was created in the Tokyo area. Over the years it grew into a group of 32 companies operating in seven segments, including e-Business, Finance and Autoworks, among others.

Yamato's star service, TA-Q-BIN, started in 1976 as a small, local parcel delivery operation for private individuals. It was Japan's first door-to-door parcel delivery service. The country has a strong gift-giving tradition. Individuals often send gifts to one another, whether on special occasions, or to distribute the many souvenirs they bring back from their travels, or for no particular reason. A substantial consumer-to-consumer delivery market was thus waiting to be fulfilled.

Several aspects differentiate Yamato from most of its competitors and helped it build its brand. First, the company focuses on the recipient who, despite having no direct business relationship with Yamato, generates most of the difficulties and disruption in the delivery process (we discuss the last mile in more detail later in this chapter). TA-Q-BIN offers a 2-hour delivery window to make it easier for recipients to be present for the delivery. Most of its competitors offer a window of 4 or 5 hours. The ability to deliver on this promise requires considerable organization and a dense delivery network.

Yamato's three precepts (Yamato n.d.a) form the core of its culture and play a decisive role in the company's success. The first one, "We all represent the company," implies that the delivery person (referred to as a Sales Driver) is expected to embody what the company stands for. The second one, "We deliver with a personal touch," is not just about ensuring parcels reach their destination but about handling these consignments with care and attention. The company's moto is "careful handling like a mother cat carries its kittens" and this is the image of its logo. The third precept, "We work with gratitude and politeness," refers to the company's role within and connection with the local community and the importance of "courtesy and moderation" in all that it does. As human resources manager Tomoki Otani explained:

> The key factor for success of our business is how the company precepts permeate every employee. ... These precepts were established in 1931 and have never changed. ... Why the company precepts are crucial for us is because they give employees core competence and judgment to respond to customers' requests flexibly. In my perspective, there are two types of skills required for the service industry. One is the basic skill such as how to drive and how to deliver. This can be learned from manuals. The other is service skill, which cannot be acquired from manuals. Underpinning service skills is the ability to judge independently in any situation without compromising the precepts. That is why we cannot provide good-quality service without correct understanding and deep conviction of the company precepts.
>
> Hwarng and Mouri (2014).

In addition, Yamato's company mission clearly prioritizes its objectives: (1) customer first; (2) safe and equal environment and opportunities for employees; (3) acting in a way that is beneficial to society (both local and in general), business and welfare (Yamato n.d.b).

The last key aspect that differentiates Yamato from other companies and has been fundamental for its success is the high-density delivery network it has built over the years in Japan. At a conference at the National University of Singapore (NUS) Business School, Makoto Kigawa, president and executive officer of Yamato Holdings Co., Ltd, stated that Yamato's last-mile delivery service could almost be considered as a kind of infrastructure like water supply, electric power and gas (NUS Business School 2012). This combination of great service and powerful principles propelled Yamato to the position of industry leader in Japan. In 2000 the company started expanding, first to Taiwan. By 2011 it had also established a presence in Singapore, Shanghai, Hong Kong and Malaysia. The challenge in all cases was the last mile. None of these countries had the delivery network that Japan had, or its gift-giving culture. In some cases the consumer-to-consumer segment did not even exist. Also, outside Japan Yamato lacked the brand awareness and trust it had built up at home over decades.

In fact, the Japanese bond with gift-giving has evolved into a strong relationship with sales drivers. Many families in Japan know who their TA-Q-BIN sales driver is and have their phone number. These drivers are invited inside Japanese homes, whereas no other stranger would be allowed to come in. The elderly, in particular, are reluctant to open their door to strangers but they have no such issue opening their door to a TA-Q-BIN sales driver.

5.3   The Fabulous Business of the Last Mile

The transport industry has been growing over the last years, riding the wave of the flourishing mail-order market, which includes e-commerce. However, companies in this sector struggle to make a profit because of the last-mile battle.

5.3.1   The Rise of the Last Mile

According to e-Marketer's *Worldwide Retail Ecommerce Sales Report* (Wurmser 2015), while the percentage of retail sales worldwide is expected to grow 5 % in total from 2013 to 2017, e-commerce sales are expected to grow between 24 % and 38 % per year over the same period. However, one country is reversing the trend. PricewaterhouseCoopers' (2015) *The Total Retail Report 2015* indicates that Switzerland is not following the global path and online shopping is decreasing in the country. One reason for this is that the Swiss do not seem to be willing to pay the cost of having parcels delivered to their homes so they browse for products online but purchase them in-store to avoid paying shipping costs. In any case, many sellers on Amazon do not even deliver to Switzerland. A couple of years ago, customers only discovered this at the end of the purchasing process, which was extremely frustrating. Now, though, customers are informed as soon as they select a product whether or not it can be shipped to their country. Similar issues were encountered on eBay. To solve the problem of so many items not being available for shipment to Switzerland, border-businesses specialized in parcel storage are growing. These enterprises, typically located in neighboring Germany or France, store parcels for shoppers, which allows Swiss consumers to purchase items that cannot be shipped to Switzerland and at the same time reduce their shipping costs (PricewaterhouseCoopers 2015). Newspaper *Le Temps* added that e-commerce sales in Switzerland are dropping because the consumer experience is not good. Customers claim that parcels arrive damaged and the logistics are inadequate, restrictive and not customer-oriented (Nikolic 2015). In the end, many Swiss customers become so disheartened with the online shopping ordeal that they give up. The example of Switzerland demonstrates the extent to which the last mile is important for logistics companies and predetermines their success.

A Morgan report (2014) shows that the size of the retail market has not changed significantly over the years but that the mail-order market has been flourishing, having doubled in the decade from 2002 to 2012. This change opens up major business opportunities for logistics companies. People are not stopping buying; they are changing the way they do so. Regardless of the channel they use to shop (Internet, catalog, etc.), what is clear is that receiving purchases by post is an expanding trend.

This landscape offers substantial opportunities for logistics companies to grow. This is one of the reasons why, despite the difficulties, Yamato expanded out of Japan. Even if it needed to change the way it worked and innovate to replace its delivery network in order to conquer new markets, the company was aware of how important it was to expand its operations abroad.

5.3.2   The Need for Scale

As we have seen, economies of scale are what drive the profitability of logistics companies, and only those with a large number of customers and a high-density network at the delivery points can be profitable. Transporting and delivering requires an infrastructure (offices, staff, warehouses), which represent fixed costs regardless of the number of clients and consignments. Companies that move large volumes are able to minimize the cost per parcel delivered. They usually send numerous packages at a time from one hub to another, which also minimizes transportation costs per item. The problem always arises in the last mile. Companies' standard shipping fees are usually based on the type of delivery (national, international), but do not take into consideration how isolated the final delivery point might be and the effort that completing the order may imply. The rates do not vary based on the real cost of the last mile, or if another journey has to be made because no one was present to take delivery of the package the first time round. Companies have been making substantial efforts to improve their first-attempt delivery rates. Mintra, India's largest e-commerce store for fashion and lifestyle products, claimed that by accepting card payments on delivery and automating its delivery process it increased its first-attempt delivery success rate from 77 to 88 % (Ezetap n.d).

Altogether, the last mile increases complexity and costs for logistics firms. Only those that move huge volumes over short distances can survive such a difficult environment. To succeed, they have to first build their network. Yamato's key advantage in Japan is its high-density network. New entrants with a similar business model need to invest to build their network, and until they have done that, they have to be prepared to lose money.

Figure 5.1 illustrates this need for scale. When companies design their product portfolio they need to consider leveraging their delivery network, knowing that some products will bring profit, some will waste it and others will represent more of an investment to help build the network. A newcomer wishing to start a courier company that connects business areas will only capitalize on its investment of hiring a person to cover a particular route once it has many customers paying to use it. The two axes in the figure show the two options that logistics companies need to opt for when managing their money. The horizontal axis is about building the network, the vertical one is about leveraging it.

Fig. 5.1 The need for scale

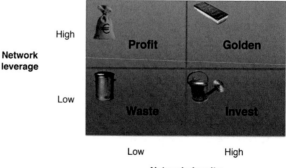

5.4   The Money in the Last-Mile Battle

For traditional logistics companies to make a profit they must leverage the delivery network they have built. Figure 5.2 looks at where Yamato's products and services are situated in the matrix and how profitable they are. Among the different services that Yamato offers, TA-Q-BIN is one of its most successful from a recognition and market implementation viewpoint (high network density, low leverage). This door-to-door parcel service is unique because of its dense delivery network and presence in the daily lives of Japanese citizens. Everybody in Japan is familiar with the brand and logo. Sales drivers are welcome inside people's homes and highly considered within the company and, as an extension, within society. TA-Q-BIN leverages the company's network but is not the most profitable service because as a C2C service, it has to be affordable for individuals.

Yamato leverages its network and the brand awareness it built through TA-Q-BIN with other, more profitable, services (high network density, high leverage). In Japan, public transport is not suitable for passengers traveling with luggage so travelers are expected to have their suitcases sent by courier. Similarly, golf players, prefer not to carry their gear themselves when they go to the course so Yamato does it for them. This is a luxury service with a higher margin than TA-Q-BIN and it is therefore more profitable. It also contributes to improving the company's delivery network.

Yamato's other services generate more added value as well as higher revenue but they are less effective at building the network. Its high household penetration and brand awareness makes it easier for its employees to access places and people that others cannot. For example, Yamato offers to visit the elderly and assist them in their daily needs, because it knows that its drivers would experience little resistance in entering these people's homes. An additional, and sometimes complementary, service is collecting broken items such as coffee machines from private homes and dropping them off for repair, then bringing the fixed item back to its owner.

Many organizations are working on innovative ideas to find better ways to compete in the last mile. Supermarkets are good at it because customers take care of the real last mile themselves. Yet 15 % of shopping malls are predicted to fail in

Fig. 5.2 Yamato example

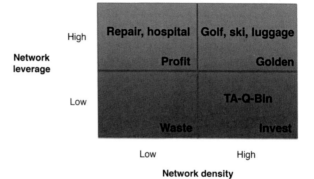

the next 10 years (Peterson 2014). This shows that the trend is changing (except in Switzerland) and customers are increasingly less willing to cover the last mile themselves.

5.5   Traditional Versus New Last-Mile Business Models: Big Data Challenges and Opportunities

In Chap. 4 we described two imagined futures a decade from now. These depend on the evolution of the omnichain and its impact on companies, markets and consumers. This section analyzes how big data may impact the logistics industry in the future. We start with traditional companies like Yamato, looking at where they stand today and exploring the evolutive (2001: A Space Odyssey) and disruptive (Blade Runner) futures with examples of new trends.

5.5.1   Big Data in the Traditional Industry Last Mile

We have seen that one of Yamato's key differentiators is its high-density network. As positive and beneficial as the company's strong network is in Japan, it did not help much when the company tried to expand to other countries.

At the core of the network is the sales driver (SD), whose role stretches far beyond delivering parcels to encompass all the work related to the operations, including delivery, pickup, collection of payment and customer service (Hwarng and Mouri 2014).

In the morning, the SD decides on the most efficient route to deliver as many parcels as possible in the shortest time without compromising safety. On this basis, he plans the loading of the vehicle, and delivers and collects parcels, if necessary advising customers on packaging for example. The sales drivers are expected to check their personal grooming and appearance before each delivery. Yamato called this type of know-how (i.e., the SD's ability to plan his route, load the truck, and deal with clients and other members of staff) "value networking." It could not replicate it in other countries, yet without it the company could not succeed abroad. In these new markets, Yamato thus has to rely on big data to acquire the special know-how of its Japanese SDs.

Yamato needs to extract from big data the knowledge that its sales drivers acquired over many years working in the field. There are three things that sales drivers master: the map of the city and its best and fastest routes, the delivery route order, and recipients' schedules. Big data provides all the information regarding the city map, traffic congestion, best routes and alternative circuits to deliver the parcels as efficiently as possible. It is thus a crucial input for working out the best delivery routes by combining information about traffic and suggesting the best options in each case, and incorporating information about receivers' schedules and habits to ensure the delivery is efficient.

Other transportation companies have already started doing what Yamato is just beginning to build outside Japan. They have all equipped their vehicles with GPSs to collect data and improve routes and delivery times. But although Yamato is lagging behind as far as big data is concerned, it has the know-how required to build and manage a high-density network, something its competitors do not have.

Therefore, as soon as Yamato has collected the big data it needs to be able to replicate the sales drivers' "value networking," it will be easier for the company to build the best infrastructure for delivering parcels. When that happens, its competitors will likely struggle to follow.

5.5.2   The Last Mile in the *2001: A Space Odyssey* Future

The 2001: A Space Odyssey future proposed a slow and progressive evolution characterized by the emergence of new models that build on what companies already have.

Delivery companies like Spanish Yupick! have already started moving in this direction by building a network of delivery points with extended opening hours, including on Sundays and bank holidays, so customers have a great deal of flexibility in picking up their packages when it is most convenient for them. Yupick! partnered with Boyaca, a logistics company specialized in delivering press. Boyaca uses its network to ship products to the final delivery point, usually a kiosk or press shop, which in Spain are open 7 days a week (Jimenez 2013).

When completing an online purchase, customers can select Yupick! as their delivery option. This costs less than delivery by a traditional courier because customers carry out part of the last-mile delivery by collecting their package from a Yupick! point. Yupick! is thus leveraging existing delivery networks and pickup points to offer a new service to customers, who pay Yupick! to have their parcels delivered to their chosen point.

Similarly, SmartCenter, Canada's largest developer of shopping centers, created Pinguinpickup points as part of its offering. Online shoppers on any Canadian website can select the most convenient Pinguinpickup point for the delivery, for which they pay the regular delivery fee. Pinguinpickup does not charge customers anything for this service, but users have to register for the service. Whereas Yupick! earns its income from the fee paid by customers, Pinguinpickup has an indirect profit formula in that the shopping malls where the pickup points are located attract additional potential customers who may not have visited the shopping center otherwise.

5.5.3   The Last Mile in the Blade Runner Future

The Blade Runner future suggests a different reality. Companies realize that their current business management models are no longer valid because they cannot handle the data and granularity of today's reality. New competitors emerge with business models architected around value generated by big data and offer new solutions to new problems.

This is the case of innovative players like Uber. The company's network consists of individuals who apply to be drivers using their own vehicles. Uber's initial app was only for individuals looking to hook up with a private driver for a specific route. Today, the company is leveraging its know-how to offer delivery services.

UberRUSH is a bicycle courier service based in New York City. It promises to collect a package within 10 minutes of an order being placed and deliver it anywhere in Manhattan. Users can track their package in real time and share the tracking map with others. Uber's delivery guarantee is that if nobody is available to receive the item, UberRUSH will bring it back to the sender. In this case Uber leveraged its existing business model to offer a new service to its customers.

Uber has also developed another new line of business, which it initially tested in Barcelona. UberEATS is a food delivery service that collects orders from selected restaurants and delivers them to the customer's door within 10 minutes (LeTart 2015). Unlike Yamato and traditional players that base their delivery services on their urban network infrastructure, Uber operates with a different business model. It relies on a network of external drivers for deliveries, so it does not have an infrastructure to maintain and can thus be much cheaper.

The question now is whether Uber, a 100 % big data company, will be able to make money in the delivery industry. Industry players agree that the smartphone era is creating new consumers who want their products delivered immediately. Traditional companies like Fedex, which offers same-day delivery in 20 countries, think that most customers do not mind waiting a day or two to receive their parcels. Uber sees a high potential in this new business, although the company admits that it is still experimenting different business models in search of one that is both efficient and profitable. Delivering food brings with it new challenges, like keeping the food warm during transport, or parking illegally to collect the food or while waiting for the client to pick it up. Sometimes drivers spend 30 minutes on a delivery that is paid just $4.99 (Macmillan 2015).

Postmates, a San Francisco-based local delivery company founded in 2011 to provide same-day delivery within the city, has now expanded to many other US cities. Its business model is based on the use of big data and bike couriers who are independent contractors and usually charge $5 to $20 per delivery. To compete with new entrants like Uber it launched its $1 deliveries in under an hour, which they hope will work when "couriers can pick up and deliver multiple items to nearby destinations—for example, pizza to a college dorm during 'Monday Night Football' games" (Macmillan and Bensinger 2015). The only way for Uber to succeed in this kind of environment would be for it to be able to combine multiple deliveries to capitalize on its drivers' deliveries.

5.6   Big Data: The Science-Fiction Future of the Last-Mile Battle

There are already numerous good intentions and ideas aimed at winning the last-mile battle, many of which are promising. But they are still a long way from becoming a reality. We know that big data can change the way the logistics industry works. It has already done so. The Internet of Things, which connects all devices to the Internet, can feed transport companies with all the information they need to track every home, parcel or any given situation imaginable.

One of the services that Caterpillar offers its customers is to work with dealers to increase uptime and reduce the operating costs of machines. Caterpillar machines are equipped with tracking devices to monitor their location, fuel consumption and utilization as well as health and maintenance issues such as those linked to hours, fluid contamination, etc. (CAT n.d.). Caterpillar knows where all its machines are at any time and even if customers are having their machines repaired by a competitor.

Having devices connected to the Internet implies that these devices can automatically take action. Suppose your refrigerator were programmed to detect when you were running out of milk and placed an order automatically. You would never run out of milk again. Samsung announced at the beginning of 2015 that 90 % of its devices will be connected to the web by 2017 and all of them by 2020. This means everything it produces, from industrial equipment to cooking devices, will be equipped with tracking systems (Swartz 2015).

5.6.1   Anticipating Consumer Behavior

With its patented Anticipatory Shipping, Amazon is anticipating consumer's purchases. The idea behind this concept is that the company sends products that it expects a customer will buy in the short term to a destination close to the final delivery area before the purchase has effectively been made. To be able to predict which products customers are likely to buy, Amazon relies on big data based on a combination of previous orders, product searches, wish lists, shopping-cart contents or how long the Internet user's cursor hovers over an item (Bensinger 2014).

Amazon is also exploring alternative ways to deliver its parcels. One of them, also patented, involves using drones. This new system revolutionizes the home delivery concept because it is no longer a home-delivery option but what they call the "bring it to me" option, which implies that buyers can receive packages wherever they are within 30 minutes of placing an order (Marsh 2015). The way it is conceived, users will select the "bring to me" option when they place an order. The smartphone's GPS will send the user's location coordinates to the drone. If the user changes location, the drone will update the delivery location based on the new coordinates received from the GPS and deliver the parcel to the new address instead. At the time of writing, this new idea was being considered as an experiment that still required multiple tests and permissions to become a reality. But it could happen earlier than we think.

In 2010 headlines claiming that Visa could predict divorces hit the news. Big data revealed that individuals who are on the verge of divorcing are more likely to miss payments and spend their money on new purchases (Ciarelli 2010). One year earlier, American Express was already offering some of its customers $300 to cancel their credit cards because the information at its disposal suggested these clients could bring more problems than benefits to the company (Pilon 2009).

Predicting consumer behavior is interesting for every company because key events such as a pregnancy and the birth of a baby, a marriage or a move usually bring about considerable changes and new selling opportunities that nobody, including logistics companies, wants to miss out on.

5.6.2   New Entrants

In this world of blurred industry boundaries, it is easy to imagine that logistics will continue to see new entrants. The evolutive and disruptive futures of Boyaca, Yupick!! and Uber prove that there is still room for change.

Amazon started as an online bookshop. Today you can purchase just about anything on Amazon and some of its new delivery patents are ahead of those of logistics companies, even though Amazon is not a logistics company. Or not yet. Or not only.

Uber is also entering the delivery industry using a new cost-reducing business model that makes its value proposition more appealing for retailers in search of affordable ways of sending their products to customers. Uber's low-cost model makes the last mile more affordable. And since retailers know that Uber is constantly innovating and looking for better and cheaper ways of doing things, linking their name to Uber's may not only help them financially but also place them at the forefront of the latest trends (LeTart 2015).

5.7   Conclusions

The trends that have emerged over the past years are greatly affecting the transportation and logistics industry. The changes affecting economies of scale that we explored in this chapter can be extrapolated to other industries. For example, taxi companies are traditionally local, covering small geographical areas. Big data can allow these companies to evolve and move into different areas. Uber is already present in 59 countries across the globe and it is continuing to expand (see Uber.com). Users trust the company and rely on it. They know it works well in their town and feel confident that drivers will not take advantage of them even if they are not familiar with the route.

Going back to the logistics industry, the battle still focuses on the last mile: the most expensive, the most complicated and, often, the longest. The first company to figure out how to minimize its cost and maximize its effectiveness will be the winner. Big data plays an important role in this battle because it equips players with the tools to make a difference.

The dependency of e-commerce on parcel distribution has turned companies that were initially conceived as online retailers into major logistics players. This is the case of Amazon, which continues to innovate and patent what today resembles science-fiction delivery methods that could well become a reality in the not-so-distant future.

Everything is transforming. The value chain is continuously gaining importance. In a few years, the logistics business may have completely changed. Big data will reinvent it and transmute it into something new. Many companies support this statement as they work on a new promising future. However, contrary to other industries where big data has already arrived and brought deep transformations, logistics companies continue to praise the beauty of big data without making realistic progress. Why is this so? As obvious and easy as it may seem to implement big data in the logistics industry, the truth is that its ecosystem is massive and is made up of multiple players. In order to make big data work, all the players would need to agree and take concerted action. Other industries, such as insurance or healthcare, have been able to do this, partly because their business case was more obvious than that of logistics companies but also because the initial investment and transformation required were not as extensive. There is, furthermore, still some reluctance in the logistics field to see the implementation of big data as a must, but we know that it will happen eventually. In fact, Amazon and Uber are already leading the journey by proposing different ways of addressing the last-mile challenge.

The active and promising landscape described in this chapter offers a glimpse of various successful examples of big data implementation. It is just a matter of time before it grows and spreads.

References

Bensinger, Greg. 2014. Amazon wants to ship your package before you buy it. WSJ.com, January 17. http://blogs.wsj.com/digits/2014/01/17/amazon-wants-to-ship-your-package-before-you-buy-it/?mod=e2tw. Accessed August 20, 2015.

CAT. N.d. Ccombining equipment, technology and services to help build your success. http://www.cat.com/en_US/support/operations/cat-connect-solutions.html. Accessed August 20, 2015.

Ciarelli, Nicholas. 2010. How Visa predicts divorce. The Daily Beast. April 6. http://www.thedailybeast.com/articles/2010/04/06/how-mastercard-predicts-divorce.html. Accessed August 20, 2015.

Ezetap (card payment app company) official website. "Customer Stories."

Hwarng, H. Brian and Motoka Mouri. 2014. Yamato Transport Co., Ltd.: TA-Q-BIN. National University of Singapore and Richard Ivey School of Business Foundation.

J.P.Morgan. 2014. Yamato Holdings (9064): High expectations a drag. J.P.Morgan Equity Research Report, May 20. (Based on data analysis by Japan Direct Marketing Association, METI and J.P. Morgan).

Jimenez, Rosa. 2013. Yupick! resuelve el problema de la entrega. El País. April 11. http://
    tecnologia.elpais.com/tecnologia/2013/04/11/actualidad/1365701132_534073.html. Accessed
    August 20, 2015.
LeTart, Jim. 2015. How Uber can help retail with last-mile delivery. Solutions Providers for Retail.
    April 21.
Macmillan, Douglas. 2015. The $50 billion question: Can Uber deliver? Wall Street Journal. June
    15, 2015. http://www.wsj.com/articles/the-50-billion-question-can-uber-deliver-1434422042?
    tesla=y. Accessed August 20, 2015.
Macmillan, Douglas and Greg Bensinger. 2015. Postmates raises $80 million in push toward $1
    deliveries. WSJ.com. June 25. http://blogs.wsj.com/digits/2015/06/25/postmates-raises-80-mil
    lion-in-push-toward-1-deliveries/. Accessed August 20, 2015.
Marsh, Rene. 2015. Amazon drone patent application imagines delivery that comes to you with
    one click. May 12. http://www.cnn.com/2015/05/12/politics/amazon-patent-drone-delivery/.
    Accessed August 20, 2015.
National University of Singapore Business School. 2012. Responding to disaster: Yamato TA-Q-
    BIN and Japan's 2011 tsunami." Video of presentation. https://www.youtube.com/watch?
    v=OSqDdI8Hs7w. Accessed August 20, 2015.
Nikolic, Dejan. 2015. Les suisses délaissent l'achat en ligne pour retourner dans les magasins. Le
    Temps. June 6. http://www.letemps.ch/Page/Uuid/081d0fb6-0baa-11e5-b8f6-5d331e67f11f/
    Les_Suisses_délaissent_lachat_en_ligne_pour_retourner_dans_les_magasins. Accessed August
    20, 2015.
Peterson, Hayley. 2014. America's shopping malls are dying a slow, ugly death. Business Insider.
    January   31.   http://www.businessinsider.com/shopping-malls-are-going-extinct-2014-1.
    Accessed August 20, 2015.
Pilon, Mary. 2009. American Express paying customers $300 to leave. February 23. http://blogs.
    wsj.com/wallet/2009/02/23/american-express-paying-customers-300-to-leave/tab/article/.
    Accessed August 20, 2015.
PricewaterhouseCoopers. 2015. The total retail report 2015.
Swartz, Jon. 2015. Samsung takes another step into Internet of Things. USA Today. May 14. http://
    www.usatoday.com/story/tech/2015/05/12/samsung-internet-of-things-arkit-smartthings/
    26997187/. Accessed August 20, 2015.
Wurmser, Yory. 2015. Worldwide retail ecommerce sales report: eMarketer's estimates and
    forecast, 2013–2018. January.
Yamato. N.d.(a) Introducing TA-Q-BIN and the Yamato Group. Yamato website. http://www.
    kuronekoyamato.co.jp/strategy/en/page00_05.html#Page00ConSub05. Accessed August 20, 2015.
Yamato. N.d.(b). Company mission. http://www.yamato-kk.jp/eng/company/#menu02. Accessed
    August 20, 2015.

New Business Models: Rocket Science

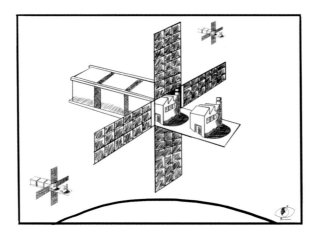

In Chap. 2 we looked at the impact that big data is having on companies' ecosystems and business models. We saw how, to take advantage of the opportunities offered by big data, companies need to adopt strategies that may vary from implementing a "digital fit" (to exploit the advantages of big data and seize the opportunities for improvement) to modifying its DNA (where the company goes through a transmutation that fundamentally changes its business model).

In this chapter we propose a four-step methodology to help you understand how your business is being transformed as a result of the big data revolution so that you can take the necessary steps to adapt it to the new reality. In each step we suggest a framework to guide the exploration and explain how it can be used. We also illustrate each step with real-life examples, including from Space Tango—a small company dedicated to launching nanosatellites into space for research purposes.

© Springer International Publishing Switzerland 2016

C. Cordon et al., *Strategy is Digital*, Management for Professionals,

DOI 10.1007/978-3-319-31132-6_6

6.1   Understanding the Context

Organizations traditionally made a product and maximized sales of it to generate a profit. However, some business models no longer follow this rule, particularly those emerging as a result of the big data revolution. Zuora CEO Tien Tzuo told *Fortune* magazine (Tzuo 2015):

> Let's look at how business has been taught for the past 100 years. It is a truth universally acknowledged that the fundamental goal of business is to create a hit product. You then sell as many units of that product, thereby spreading your fixed costs over as many units as you can, and you compete on margins. Well, in my opinion that's all worthless. Those days are gone.

Traditional ways of making money are becoming less applicable. Revenues and costs may be disconnected or have a non-linear relation. A good example of a company that belongs to an ecosystem in which traditional rules do not apply is Google. Its business model is characterized by the importance it places on its users and the deals the company establishes with advertisers. For example, it earns money with Google Maps in two different ways: first, through a B2C model where individuals and businesses can advertise on its website maps.google.com (using programs such as AdSense and AdWords); second, through a B2B model where companies can integrate Google Maps into their own services and purchase a license to do so. At the beginning of the B2B service, that license was quoted as costing thousands of dollars, but now it is free for a certain number of map uploads per day, and beyond that the cost depends on the number of daily map uploads. This is similar to Google's strategy for other products such as Gmail, where a version with limited functionalities is available for free and a version with additional functionalities is available for a fee.

Another major trend is that industry boundaries are blurring. Until recently, they were relatively well defined and it was clear to which industry a company belonged based on what it made, such as watches, cars, mobile phones, etc. Today, this is not always so clear-cut. Apple, for example, started out making computers but then moved on to also produce smartphones, watches and digital media players. Rumors suggest that the company might even be considering entering the car industry. Thus, although Apple started out in the computer industry, it now competes in several others, including telecommunications and watches, and possibly soon in the automobiles.

In this blurring industry landscape, organizations are evolving toward unknown territories where the ecosystem plays an increasingly important role. To compete, companies need to think hard and deep about their purpose and future direction.

6.2   Four Steps to Adapt to the Changing Landscape

Crucial questions that companies need to consider as they embark on their journey to adapt to the big data movement and compete in a blurry industry landscape are:

- Why does the company exist?
- How will its business model look in the big data era?
- What is its profit formula?
- How should the strategy be executed?

These are the questions that we aim to help you answer in the following section using our four-step methodology.

The four steps are summarized in Fig. 6.1. The first question to ask is, "WHY" does the company exist? We propose to use Simon Sinek's Golden Circle to address this. The second question is, "HOW" do I make the change suggested as an outcome of the first step? We introduce a simplified business map inspired by Osterwalder and Pigneur's (2010) business model canvas to help us in this task. The canvas (or map) is useful for understanding and capturing in a snapshot how a company functions. The third question is, "WHAT" needs to be done to improve and maximize the company's profit? We use the profit formula tool to work this out. Finally, we look at how to execute the new business strategy more efficiently and successfully using the principles of Lean Startup. Part of the Lean Startup concept is to always measure and collect feedback and learn from it, repeating the process again and again as a cycle aimed at adapting to customers' needs.

Fig. 6.1 A four-step model to adapting companies to the changing landscape

6.2.1 WHY: Defining the Company's Purpose

Mediq—the major Dutch healthcare company discussed in detail in Chap. 3 and referred to in other chapters—used to be just a drug retailer and distributor. Its profits initially came from the fees it earned on the medicines it sold. In 2012 the Dutch government deregulated pharmaceutical fees, resulting in an immediate 90% drop in the company's profits. It had to rethink its business model.

Under the leadership of a new CEO, the top management team transformed the company's main mission from packaging and distributing medicines and medical supplies to looking after patients. To do so, it designed a new business model with new key drivers: improving the quality of life of patients and avoiding unnecessary hospitalizations. Big data made this possible. An external company used big data to estimate the yearly hospital admissions per patient and the total cost this represented for insurance companies. Mediq proposed to drastically reduce these expenses. By knowing its customers, tracking their medical treatments and offering advice on their use, it could avoid hospitalizations due to incorrect use of medicines. The savings achieved with this approach are split between the insurers and Mediq and represent half of Mediq's total profits.

The purpose of Mediq's existence changed when it considered its WHY. As a result, the company's business model, mission and the way it made its money and products changed too.

Like Mediq, many companies have based their selling arguments on what they do. Simon Sinek (2009) developed his "Golden Circle" (see Fig. 6.2) to guide companies through the process of shifting their focus from WHAT they do to WHY they do it in order to define their purpose. Sinek's Golden Circle helps visualize why some companies are successful and others making similar products are not.

- The external circle is the WHAT: It refers to the product a company makes or the service it offers. An automobile company might say, "We sell great cars." This is the kind of message that organizations usually convey to their customers.
- The second circle is the HOW: It is about the company's purpose and explains the way the company works and does things. Some companies are already communicating at this level.
- The third circle is the WHY. It represents the company's emotional hook and, as Sinek (2009) put it, it asks, "Why should anyone care?"

Traditionally, companies have communicated from the outside in, starting by explaining what they do, how they do it and, occasionally (most of the time companies do not know), why they do it. A hardware company following this model might articulate its message as follows:

Fig. 6.2 Simon Sinek's
Golden Circle

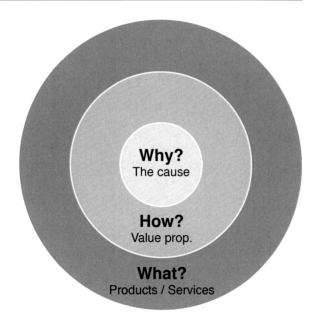

- WHAT?—We make great computers.
- HOW?—They are beautify designed and user friendly. Do you want to buy one?
- WHY?—(Companies often do not know and thus do not answer this question)

Sinek proposes to reverse the order and start communicating with customers from the WHY to the HOW then to the WHAT. What matters to today's consumers is not so much the type of product or service that companies sell, but the reason they are doing so. They want to know the purpose of the company and feel engaged with what they are purchasing. They want the act of buying to become a complete and fulfilling experience. The only way for companies to satisfy that wish is to tell consumers WHY they are doing what they do. In a TED Talk, Sinek (2009) emphasized that consumers are not interested in what companies do, but WHY they are doing it. Why is Apple so successful, and so different from its competitors? It sells smartphones and computers that are not so different technically from other devices. What it does do differently, though, is to communicate its WHY to its customers (Sinek 2009):

- WHY?—We believe in challenging the status quo in everything we do; we believe in thinking differently.
- HOW?—The way we challenge the status quo is by designing attractive and user-friendly products.
- WHAT?—We just happen to make computers. Do you want to buy one?"

People buy products for the same reason they follow leaders: they feel inspired by them.

Mediq used to work and relate to its customers on the basis of its WHAT, i.e. moving boxes from hand to hand. It had never wondered WHY it did this. It was only when faced with an extreme situation that it started to look outside its boundaries and revisit its purpose, and only then did it realize that its real purpose could be far more relevant and transcendent. This brought about fundamental changes in Mediq's business model. From being industry driven it moved to being socially driven. From "Expensive if possible, cheap when necessary" it shifted to "Expensive when necessary, cheap if possible." It acquired the necessary competencies to serve its new customers and achieve its goals. In sum, it underwent a complete transmutation, including in the way it made its money—its profit formula.

Sinek's WHY framework could be instrumental in the big data transformation process of many companies wishing to follow the example of Mediq by revisiting their purpose.

Sometimes a company's WHY has more personal roots, as in the case of Space Tango.

Space Tango used space to discover, design and commercialize solutions related, among other things, to healthcare on planet Earth. Its WHAT was to send nanosatellites into space. In 2014 the company focused on marketing and commercializing the entrepreneurial space marketplace. Space Tango CEO Twyman Clements experienced serious health problems while growing up and he believed that Space Tango's space mission (its WHY) could, among other things, help advance medical discoveries on Earth. Twyman explained using a personal example:

My immediate answer comes from a device that literally hasn't left my side in more than a decade. The core technology of the insulin pump I use to regulate my glucose levels as a Type I diabetic was initially developed for the Viking landers that were sent to Mars in the late 1970s. I can actually say the effect of our space economy is in my blood. (Twyman, quoted in Cordón and Lennox 2015).

Carrying out experiments with the objective of seeking to improve other people's lives was a strong motivator, and he wholeheartedly believed that Space Tango could improve people's health through technology research or by fostering the development of exomedicine.[1] This WHY was engraved in the company's DNA and widely shared with everybody, including employees, customers and investors.

---

[1] According to Wikipedia, exomedicine is the study and exploration of medical solutions in the zero gravity environment of space to promote benefits to human health on Earth.

6.2.2 HOW: Visualizing the Company's Ecosystem

Having articulated the company's WHY, the next step is to visualize and synthesize the company and its ecosystem. A useful framework to do this is Osterwalder's Business Model Canvas, which serves to view the company as a whole and connect all the dots around it.

6.2.2.1 The Business Model Canvas

Osterwalder originally proposed his Business Model Canvas (see Fig. 6.3) as a tool for new technological startups that needed to be able to explain easily to investors how they worked and where they would make their money (Osterwalder and Pigneur 2010). Osterwalder started his research on business models in 2000, just after the dotcom bubble had burst and these types of companies needed help. He published his findings in his doctoral thesis in 2004 (Osterwalder 2004) then continued to develop his ideas, creating and publishing the Business Model Canvas in 2010.

One of the first things that Osterwalder realized while he was working on his book was that "you can't write a book about business model innovation without an innovative business model" (Osterwalder 2011). *Business Model Generation* is the outcome of implementing a revolutionary business model based on crowd funding, co-creation and self-publishing. He asked a group of people to help him financially on the book and take part in something huge that would allow them all to learn from one another. They joined a hub that was fed with information about the book, and

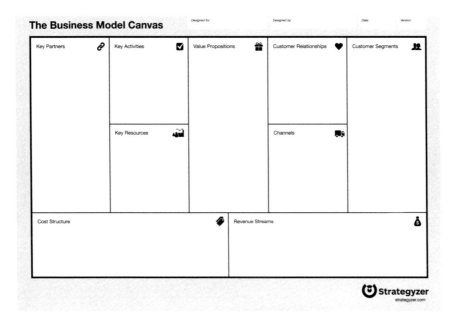

Fig. 6.3 Osterwalder's business model canvas (Strategyzer n.d.)

their names were included in the final product, which was published through a self-printing and -distribution company.

A company may have more than one business model in which case it will develop as many canvases. However, as the number of business models increases, the complexity of managing the company increases exponentially. Experience shows that companies cannot handle more than a few business models at a time.

In parallel to the work developed by Osterwalder, other authors built on the business model concept by adding the profit formula. In an article entitled "Reinventing your business model," Johnson (2008) reviewed and highlighted the importance of the new business models in reshaping industries and companies. According to the authors, a business model starts with the value proposition—the way the company creates value for its customers—and should always include a **profit formula**. The key resources (people, technology, products, facilities, equipment, channels and brand) and processes are the other two elements that should be part of every model.

6.2.2.2 A Visually Simplified Canvas

Building on Osterwalder's Business Model Canvas and the proposal in the article "Reinventing your business model," we developed a simplified canvas, or business map, with just three sections to differentiate three concepts: Internal resources, information about customers and the way the company wants to make money—the value proposition (see Fig. 6.4).

The development of this new map was driven by the need to make the business model easier to understand at a glance and, at the same time, simple to explain. The three sections are:

- The **key elements.** This box groups together the key resources, partners and processes, which together determine the way the company operates:
  - The **resources** include everything that is needed to make a product: the team, the factory, the brands, intellectual property, etc.

Fig. 6.4 A simplified business model canvas: The Map

The map

Key resources	Customer value proposition:
Key partners	Value offered to the market
	Segment of customers
Key processes	Communication and distribution channel
	Relationship with clients
Profit formula: Revenue streams, pricing, cost structure	

- – The **partners** are companies that the organization will work with and interact with to deliver its product(s) or service(s). They are mainly suppliers but can also include firms that the organization may interact and collaborate with in the ecosystem.
- – The **processes** are the way in which the organization generates its product (s) or service(s). These can include the purchase-to-pay process, the order-to-delivery process, the order-to-cash process, etc. They also encompass other functions such as training, development, etc.
- The **customer value proposition.** This describes the value that a company brings to the market as well as all the elements that relate to communication, customer segmentation and the relationship with partners.
- The **profit formula.** This synthesizes the elements that are used as key indicators to create the profit formula, such as the revenue stream, pricing and the cost structure. The profit formula is discussed in more detail in Sect. 6.3.

A business map is especially useful for companies needing to make important decisions with regard to their strategies because it draws a clear and realistic picture of the company and its situation. We illustrate hereafter the type of situation in which a business map can help in decision making using a case study from Space Tango.

6.2.2.3 Space Tango's Business Model Canvas

When Space Tango decided to look for funding, its CEO was overwhelmed by the difficulties he encountered in trying to attract venture capitalists. Twyman knew that before he could attend any meetings with potential investors, he needed to be able to explain clearly and concisely two concepts: what his company's business was and how it was going to make its money. As he said:

Since I got the CEO job, my biggest challenge is making sure we focus on the right things and get the right message out. Obviously, the end goal is the money, but the right message is a subset of that. It's good that I come from the technical side because I can answer all the technical questions, but I explain everything like an engineer rather than from the customer's perspective. My big worry is learning how to pitch Space Tango fast enough so that we don't get passed up. I think we've got a really good idea, and I don't want to be saying in a few months, "Damn it, we messed up." (Twyman, quoted in Cordón and Lennox 2015)

The business map helped Twyman synthesize Space Tango's business model to make it understandable for everybody and easy to share with investors. It included an analysis of Space Tango's ecosystem, which was fundamental to understand the overall company and its purpose.

However, one difficulty that Twyan encountered was fathoming how to make money out of the company's great idea of using small satellites to make

(continued)

> *anti-gravity experiments that would produce life-saving learnings. The profit*
> *formula was essential to explain how Space Tango could make money*
> *implementing its business model.*[2]

6.2.3 WHAT: Finding the Best Profit Formula

The business model canvas helps companies quickly understand their business
model and synthesize how they work. The profit formula goes a step further by
helping to clarify how the company makes money. For example, will its revenues
come from traditional sources? Or has the company developed new successful ways
of earning revenue that were not being given enough attention? Is there just one
profit formula or are there several? The profit formula is also valuable for comparing different business models and helping choose the best one.

Traditional companies that manufactured physical products and used cost
accounting to work out their margin had a simple profit formula. All they needed
to worry about was the price of the raw materials and the margin they wanted to
earn. Today things are not so straightforward. As Tien Tzuo explained in an
interview with *Fortune* magazine, not all of today's companies sell physical
products—some offer online services and others have multiple sources of revenue.

> *Before it reinvented itself, Mediq earned its income from its margins on the*
> *medicines it sold. The shift in the company's purpose and business model*
> *fundamentally transformed its profit formula from a single traditional one to*
> *two new contradicting profit formulas. The first one was based on the fees it*
> *made on the medicines it sold but the second one was based on the savings*
> *achieved by keeping its clients healthy. Over time, 50 % of the company's*
> *profits came from the second one, so from a financial point of view, both*
> *formulas were well balanced.*

The Mediq example shows that companies can apply a variety of profit formulas
to succeed. The key is to find the best one (or ones) for a particular company and its
business model.

6.2.3.1 The Traditional Profit Formula
The profit formula concept is not new. Also known as the DuPont Analysis, it has
been used for many years to find the best way to make businesses profitable.
However, fresh opportunities are being created in the fast-changing environment
we now live in and these require different profit formulas to adapt to the specific
needs and numbers. The traditional DuPont formula is, in many cases, no longer
applicable.

---

[2] For more information about Space Tango's business model canvas, see Cordón and
Lennox (2015).

Fig. 6.5 Profit formula (DuPont analysis) for a traditional business

$$ROE = \frac{Netincome}{Sales} \times \frac{Sales}{Assets} \times \frac{Assets}{Equity}$$

$$ROE = Margin \times Assetturnover \times Leverage$$

Named after DuPont, the company that first started using it in the 1920s, it is normally used for traditional businesses, regardless of their size.

In a traditional business like bread-making for example, the bread manufacturer will first try to maximize the return on his investment.

It is a truth universally acknowledged that the fundamental goal of business is to create a hit product. You then sell as many units of that product, thereby spreading your fixed costs over as many units as you can, and you compete on margins (Tzuo 2015).

Maximizing the return on investment (ROI) is achieved by increasing sales and decreasing costs. Figure 6.5 shows a traditional profit formula, which first tries to maximize the margin obtained from the total sales of bread. This is obtained by dividing the net income by the sales. The higher the number, the greater the margin earned by the bread manufacturer.

Second, the bread manufacturer will focus on making as much bread as possible with the machines (assets) he has. If the manufacturer has more than one factory, he will want each one to produce and sell as much as possible. This is the asset turnover, which is calculated by dividing the sales by the value of its assets.

Finally, the bread manufacturer will need to take into account the debts (or leverage) on his factories, which is calculated by dividing the assets by the equity.[3]

> *A bread manufacturer can be compared to a small bakery. Both could have the same return on equity. A bread manufacturer selling inexpensive bread in supermarkets will usually have a low margin but a large number of sales. The product quality is not expected to be high, because the selling argument is mainly the price. In contrast, a small bakery that bakes its own bread in a wood-burning oven using top-quality organic ingredients will produce fewer units but will sell each one at a higher price. Its production costs are expected to be high, but the higher price of the final product should cover the additional cost, and the small bakery's margins should still surpass those of the larger, mass-production bread manufacturer. The baker's asset turnover, however, will be much lower.*

---

[3] In order to simplify the explanation of the profit formula, from now on we will leave aside the "leverage" because it adds complexity and does not help clarify the concepts we are reviewing in this chapter.

Fig. 6.6 Profit formula of a software company

$$ROE = \frac{Revenue}{Licence} \times \frac{\# Licences}{Softwareproduct} \times \frac{\# Softwareproduct}{Invest.} \times \left(\frac{Invest.}{Equity}\right)$$

$$ROE = Marginperlicence \times Numberoflicences \times Numberofsoftware$$

This traditional formula is useful for comparing businesses that are similar but positioned differently in the market and it demonstrates how changing the numbers in the formula can yield a comparable profit (return on equity).

> *Among the brands that the Swatch Group owns are the popular Swatch brand and the luxury Omega brand. How does the company compare the results of both companies? Omega watches yield a high margin per product but a low asset turnover because everything is handmade in Switzerland. Swatch's margin per unit is low but the company can produce many more watches per factory because it has automated the manufacturing process, therefore its asset turnover is high. Thus the same formula reveals different results for each type of product and allows the company to make comparisons.*

Things become more complicated when this traditional formula is applied to other industry sectors. For example, it would not make sense for a software company to use this formula because a computer program is made once but may be sold millions of times. The concept of margin and net income over sales would not be a valid indicator, because issuing a new license for the software does not cost anything, unlike manufacturing a physical product. The software company's profit formula would be similar to the one in Fig. 6.6. Its return on equity will be based on the revenue it earns on each license, the number of licenses sold per software product, and the number of software products created. In the case of Microsoft Windows, the company first tries to sell its licenses at the highest possible price. Then, with each additional license that it sells, the greater the margin it earns per license because its initial cost in developing the product is spread across more licenses. In addition, Microsoft may want to maximize its portfolio of products to increase its offering for different clients.

6.2.3.2 The Profit Formula of the Consulting Industry

The profit formula applied to consultants where the partners own the company is different again (see Fig. 6.7). Their objective is to maximize their return on each partner (ROPartner) so they play with the margin they obtain per consultant, with the sales that each consultant makes and with the number of consultants per partner.

Comparing the consultant and guru profit formulas demonstrates how changing the profit formula will change the strategy. Although these three types of consultancy business might use the same equation, the different values of their parameters produce distinct profit formulas. Both the guru and the consultant want to make as

Fig. 6.7 Profit formula of consultants and gurus

$$ROPartner = \frac{Netincome}{Sales} \times \frac{Sales}{Consultant} \times \frac{Consultant}{Partner}$$

$$Revenue\ per\ partner = Margin \times Load \times Ratio$$

Organization	Margin	Load	Ratio
Outsourced	Low	High	High
Consultant	High	Medium	Medium
Guru	Very high	Low	Low

much money as possible, but they have to do it differently because the guru's time constraints are not the same as those of the consultant's. Yet this time constraint is precisely what justifies that the guru can command a higher margin per activity.

6.2.3.3 Different Profit Formulas in the Same Company

A company may have different business models that are incompatible with each other. In this case it usually handles each one as it if were a different company and may even separate them physically.

> *Fiat has owned Ferrari since 1969. They both share the same objective of selling cars. But their products are completely different, as are their profit formulas. Fiat sells affordable cars to regular consumers. Its strategy is based on low prices, high volumes of sales and low margins. Ferrari sells brand exclusivity and its luxury cars yield high margins. The objective of both organizations is to maximize their revenue, but whereas Fiat does so by selling a high number of units, Ferrari does so by increasing its margins. In 2013 Ferrari reported record revenues despite intentionally selling fewer cars (Foy 2014). Later that year, after changing CEOs, the company decided to increase its production to "keep pace with the super-rich" (Ebhardt 2014). Fiat and Ferrari use the same profit formula equation but emphasize different parameters in their pursuit of profitability.*

6.2.3.4 Applying Disparate Profit Formulas in the Same Ecosystem

Devoting time to analyze the profit formulas of other players in the ecosystem is important to understand where they stand. Often, partners fail to reach an agreement in a negotiation because both want to protect the way they make their money without considering the business model of the other.

A software company may partner with distributors to sell licenses. The problems arise when both parties have different interests. The software company wants to sell as many licenses as possible, but the partner (Fig. 6.8) may be more interested in selling a maximum number of consulting and development hours to final clients to implement the software products in their companies because they can earn much more from that than from reselling the software license.

Fig. 6.8 Profit formula of a software company partner

$$ROE = \frac{Revenue}{Hour} \times \frac{\# Hours}{Consultant} \times \frac{\# Consultants}{Invest.} \times \left(\frac{Invest.}{Equity}\right)$$

$$ROE = Marginperhour \times Workload \times Numberofconsultants$$

6.2.3.5 The Profit Formulas of Big Data Companies

The examples of profit formulas we have presented so far are common and illustrative but they do not relate directly to big data. The following examples aim to help explain how the profit formulas of big data companies work.

When Google started out, it did not have a clear idea of how it would make money. The founder knew that the key to success was the algorithm on which the company based its web search results. Up until then, other engines like Yahoo and Lycos had led the game, offering search results based on the number of times a word or term searched for appeared on a web page. Thus, a company selling pizzas would include the word "pizza" a hundred times or more throughout its website to ensure it would be as high as possible on the search results list.

Google changed its approach to make the user the center of the experience. It defined an algorithm that used, as one of its key parameters, the number of times that other websites referred to the website the user was searching. It combined this with geolocation information about the user. The results were those that the algorithm considered most relevant to the user based on his location. For Google, the user meant everything, and its objective was to improve its search engine and other web experiences.

> The founders ran [Google] on a few simple principles, first and foremost of which was to focus on the user. They believed that if they created great services, they could figure out the money stuff later. If all they did was create the world's best search engine, they would be very successful (Schmidt 2014).

Google Maps makes its money from the fees that companies pay to have their advertisements appear at the top of search results. The company developed a new model that was a success right from the start. It was different to the traditional model used by Yellow Pages, which earned income from selling expensive space to advertisers in its yellow telephone directories, but for which the cost did not take into account the success rate of the ad or its impact or the number of people that would see it. It was thus restricted to companies with substantial advertising budgets.

Google Maps developed a new model with completely different characteristics:

- **Customization** It customizes its advertisements based on the geographical area of the user, so only those located in the same area as the advertiser at the time of searching for something online (and who are therefore more likely to be potential customers) see the ad.

- **Budget** Google Maps charges advertisers a small fee each time someone clicks on their ad, so local businesses only pay a relatively small amount on customized ads and they can directly measure their impact. They can also fix a maximum budget that they want to spend on advertising.
- **Flexibility** Advertisers can opt for a variety of pay-per-click options with different fees. If an advertiser activates the "how to get there" option, it will pay a specified amount every time a user clicks on that button.
- **Real-time updates** Advertisers can update their information any time.

To maximize its profits Google Maps can play with three parameters: the amount it earns per clicked ad, the number of ads it shows in each search, and the total number of searches per dollar invested (see Fig. 6.9).

Google based its initial strategy on making its services an interesting experience for the advertiser by offering the basic service of appearing on Google Maps free of charge. Advertisers wishing to improve the user experience could pay to increase their relevance on Google Maps, which increased Google's revenue per ad. Google's goal is to maximize the number of regular users to boost the number of searches. The more Google Maps is used, the more the company earns.

Uber developed a smartphone app to connect drivers with passengers for private transport at a lower rate than normal taxis. The app provides an estimate of the cost of the ride upfront, before the passenger calls the car. The fare can be split with other passengers. Uber retains 20 % of each ride (Marx 2015), the rest is for the driver. Uber's profit formula focuses on maximizing the number of trips by boosting the number of both passengers and drivers (see Fig. 6.10). Of course, the more it earns per ride, the better, but distance is not as straightforward an indicator as the number of passengers and drivers, and it is harder to measure and control.

Profit formulas are useful for understanding if actions that you are planning to undertake in your company, such as improving customer after-sales service, will affect the way you are making money or if they will cost more than they bring in.

Fig. 6.9 Profit formula for Google Maps

$$ROE = \frac{Revenue}{Ad} \times \frac{\# Clicks}{Search} \times \frac{\# Search}{Invest.} \times \left(\frac{Invest.}{Equity}\right)$$

$$ROE = Revenueperad \times \# Clickspersearch \times \# Searchper\$$$

Fig. 6.10 Profit formula of Uber

$$ROE = \frac{Revenue}{Trip} \times \frac{\# Trips}{User} \times \frac{\# User}{Invest.} \times \left(\frac{Invest.}{Equity}\right)$$

$$ROE = Revenuepertrip \times Utilization \times \# Userper\$$$

6.2.3.6 Space Tango's Profit Formula

Space Tango was born out of a great idea but it lacked a clear profit formula. It is not alone in that situation. Google's story is similar in that before knowing how it would make its money, the company focused on improving the user experience based on the belief that the rest would come later. It worked.

Space Tango's nanosatellites were a great product, but what strategy would make the company profitable?

> From Twyman's perspective, Space Tango had a services side and a product side. The services side included Space Tango's consulting services to FedEx on FedEx Space Solutions, as well as selling capability on its antenna and environmental testing systems. The capability part was not a long-term growth strategy, but it brought cash in the door. But as Twyman said, "The balancing act is when does it become a distraction."
>
> The product side was focused on the TangoLab facility that would be installed on the ISS [International Space Station] in 2015. The TangoLab platform would generate several sources of revenue. The second generation of the Lab product line would be a more biomedical-specific version. Space Tango planned to have this installed on the ISS in about 12–24 months. The vast majority of the $1 million in capital that Space Tango hoped to raise would be used for this project.
>
> There were also some small opportunities in education and research. The highest-risk, highest-return opportunity was the Exomedicine Institute, which to date had mostly been self-funded because outside sources of funding had been sporadic and small. However, once the second Lab was installed on the ISS, Space Tango hoped that the EMI could achieve its objective of working with partners to identify opportunities where exomedicine experiments might help in the fight to improve the outcome of certain diseases. (Cordón and Lennox 2015)

At first glance there were three profit formulas that Space Tango could pursue: Selling satellites, selling experiments and selling consulting services.

1. **Selling satellites** The company would obtain its revenues from each nanosatellite (CubeSat) that it sent to space. Whenever it sold one of these satellites to a company, Space Tango would manufacture it, equip it with whatever the client wanted to send to space, and make sure that the satellite was launched and placed in its orbit. Space Tango's revenues would come from its margin on the CubeSat multiplied by the number of CubeSats it sent to space (see Fig. 6.11).
2. **Selling experiments** If Space Tango opted to focus on selling experiments it would shift its focus from making CubeSats to maximizing the use of the room available in the International Space Station (ISS) to place experiments there. The company would prepare the experiments and someone else would send them to the ISS. Its profit formula would be like the one in Fig. 6.12 whereby the company would need to optimize its margin on each experiment sold and the number of experiments that it sent to the ISS.
3. **Consulting services** Space Tango's third potential source of income consisted in providing consulting services to companies. We described this profit formula earlier in the chapter when we talked about the gurus and consulting companies (see Fig. 6.6).

The dilemma that Space Tango—like many other companies—faced was not easy to resolve. The company had to decide how it would make money, which profit

Fig. 6.11 Profit formula of Space Tango Satellites

$$ROE = \frac{Revenue}{Cube} \times \frac{\#\,Cubes}{Launch} \times \frac{\#\,Launches}{Invest.} \times \left(\frac{Invest.}{Equity}\right)$$

$$ROE = Marginpercube \times Cubesperrocket \times Rocketper\$$$

Fig. 6.12 Profit formula for Space Tango experiments

$$ROE = \frac{Revenue}{Experiment} \times \frac{\#\,Experiment}{SpaceinISS} \times \frac{\#\,SpaceinISS}{Invest.} \times \left(\frac{Invest.}{Equity}\right)$$

$$ROE = Marginperexperiment \times UtilizationofISS \times ISSspaceper\$$$

formula would be the most convenient and why. There was no right or wrong decision at this point because it was impossible to know in advance which one would work best. One thing was sure, though, the chosen profit formula would influence the business model. An important point to consider was which one would be easier to understand and most likely to capture the interest of investors, without whom there would be no company.

It is always a good idea to look at the organization with the eyes of an investor, scouting for appealing concepts and easy ways to make money. Another useful tool to help decide which path to take is the Lean Startup framework discussed in Sect. 6.2.4.

6.2.4   Executing the Strategy Using Lean Startup

The next step is to implement the strategy in the most efficient way possible. One methodology that can help is Lean Startup.

Eric Ries designed his Lean Startup methodology to help startups go to market. It adapts Lean (the famous methodology introduced by Toyota to eliminate waste within a manufacturing process) to startups and their particular reality. Startups usually fail because they spend so much time perfecting a product that by the time it finally reaches the market, it fails to capture the interest of customers. Inspired by the few companies that did succeed—out of the millions that failed—Lean Startup offers a systematic approach to creating and managing startups and bring their products to market faster by eliminating wasted working time, investments, etc.

The initial product that the startup develops does not need to be perfect. On the contrary, most likely it will be basic and even unfinished (at this point it is called a minimum viable product) but good enough to fulfill its intended purpose and help the startup measure its effectiveness. The minimum viable product is a prototype that the company brings to the market to test how users or customers react. It is crucial to collect the feedback from these early adopters and learn from it. This is what Lean Startup defines as *validated learning*. It serves to improve the product

Fig. 6.13 The Lean Startup
Cycle

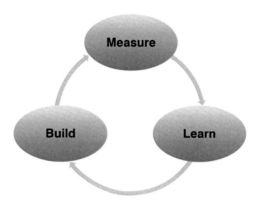

before it is made on a larger scale. The testing never ends, and the startup must measure and learn from the results of each iteration, then *pivot*, i.e. adapt the product to the new reality (see Fig. 6.13). Lean Startup is thus based on an ongoing experimentation and learning cycle.

Any organization, big or small, new or established can apply the Lean Startup methodology to implement and execute their business plan. If, like Space Tango, it wants to test several profit formulas, the Lean Startup learning cycle can be of great use. Once the company has worked out its profit formulas and put in place its strategy, it needs to experiment to learn which options of the strategy are successful and which ones should be discarded. The company can then adapt to the most successful options.

> *At Space Tango, Twyman was keen to check how the three business models and their respective profit formulas would work. The company already used 3D printing technology to design and test prototypes. Lean Startup could also be useful to test the profit formulas and see which of them best suited the company and the existing market. Twyman had to be rigorous and use the validated learning collected from testing its 3D-printed minimum viable product to improve Space Tango's nanosatellites.*

6.2.4.1 Lean Startup in Large Organizations

Lean Startup is not only for startups or small companies. Big corporations like Accenture, Coca-Cola or General Electric are also using it to increase their teams' agility, speed, focus and drive, something that such giants usually lack (Alsever 2015).

> *Coca-Cola, for example, created a new program named "Coca-Cola Founders" that combines the startup and the multinational worlds to solve problems directly connected to Coca-Cola, working with experienced*

(continued)

*entrepreneurs around the world.[4] The corporation generally takes a 20 %
equity stake in the startups, which are deployed applying the lean startup
methodology. The startups can leverage Coca-Cola's equipment, partners,
distribution channels, etc. to test, build and scale their ideas.*

*Coca-Cola Founders is the third version of an initiative that first started
and failed because, according to Coca-Cola VP of Innovation and Entre-
preneurship David Butler, "it was just a bunch of executives and managers in
a boardroom, trying to come up with innovative startup ideas. . . . The room
was filled with managers, not explorers" (Weinberger 2015). The second
version of the platform was built by in-company entrepreneurs tasked with
solving hard problems. But they were internal employees who had not
invested their own equity in their startups, and they lacked the motivation
that usually empowers startups.*

*The third version of this platform has already hatched an important number
of startups developing ideas that Coca-Cola admits could never have come
from inside the company. For example, Wonolo is a platform where companies
can announce vacancies for temporary work to be completed within approximately 24 hours. It has been defined as the "Uber for people."*

*Like Uber, Wonolo rapidly allocates the most appropriate person in the
right spot and provides unemployed or underemployed workers with a
reasonably steady source of income. The question in both cases is, will this
sharing economy platform end up jeopardizing workers on payroll? Time will
tell. Until then, the beauty of Wonolo is that it was a lean startup project
endorsed by a large multinational that brought together two worlds that
would probably never have blended a few years ago. And although Wonolo
was initially created to solve Coca-Cola problems, it can serve many
companies facing similar situations (Weinberger 2015).*

6.3   Conclusions

This chapter analyzed the impact that big data is having on companies' business
models and their ecosystems.

Today, organizations need to enter and conquer unknown territories where the
ecosystem plays an important role. The ecosystem has become such an important
aspect of company strategy that understanding what a company does, and especially
why it does it, means being able to explain its ecosystem and the role the firm plays in it.

We presented a four-step guide to embarking on the big data journey and
implementing big data in companies. Based on the experiences of organizations
that have succeeded in this journey, we proposed a methodology that combines four
different frameworks:

---

[4] For more Information, see the Coca-Cola Founders website: http://www.coca-colafounders.com.

1. **WHY** To embrace the big data revolution it is important to define the company's WHY, and start communicating it. The WHY represents the company purpose, the reason for its existence. Articulating it allows organizations to consider new unexplored business models that will be aligned with the company purpose.
2. **HOW—The business model canvas** Several new kinds of business model have been created in the past years. The way some companies make their money today is quite different from traditional models. The business model canvas (or map) is a useful tool to help synthesize and present a company's business model in a visual manner and make it easier to explain to investors.
3. **WHAT—the profit formula** The profit formula goes a step further by helping to understand how the company makes its money. We showed how juggling key parameters can reveal the best strategy for maximizing profits.
4. **EXECUTING the strategy with Lean Startup** Companies often need a framework to implement their strategy. Lean Startup proposes a cycle that starts with building a prototype—or minimum viable product—which is tested on the market. The learning acquired from the feedback is used to produce a revised prototype, which is again tested on the market in an unending cycle of building, measuring, learning, rebuilding and so forth.

Companies based on new big data business models are structured differently to traditional ones and their revenue comes from unconventional sources. Google, for example, is constantly coming up with novel business models to deliver new kinds of services. It is not always easy to see at first glance where it makes its money. When it comes to digital businesses, it is necessary to see the whole picture to really understand the company's global meaning—why the new service was created, its purpose and how it will make a profit. If we only focus on what the company does without looking at its entire ecosystem, the explanation will be biased.

The business model canvas and the profit are especially important for companies evolving in the big data ecosystem because the new business models being generated by big data are often difficult for investors, company executives and employees to understand.

As we finished writing this book, we noticed a new trend. Years ago, companies' business models were stable and remained almost untouched for years. This is the case of "traditional" companies like Nestlé, Volkswagen or Bayer. In the digital age, organizations are generating new models that do not necessarily have much to do with their existing ones. Google and Apple are exploring the possibility of entering the car industry, which has nothing to do with their current businesses. One way to evaluate if such an adventure makes sense is to use a tool like the business model canvas to verify if a diversification move of this scale would bring them a competitive advantage, or if embracing such projects would mean merely acting as an incubator.

As business models continue to evolve, the new ones bear little resemblance to the old ones. Big data is shaping and reshaping them for good, and companies need to use the tools at their disposal to continuously adapt to the new reality.

Appendix 1: IMD Case Space Tango (A)

IMD-7-1629
19.01.2015

SPACE TANGO: DANCING WITH THE STARS (A)

Researcher Beverley Lennox prepared this case under the supervision of Professor Carlos Cordón as a basis for class discussion rather than to illustrate either effective or ineffective handling of a business situation.

LEXINGTON, KENTUCKY, SEPTEMBER 2014. It was six weeks since Twyman Clements had been named president and CEO of Space Tango, the newly established for-profit, marketing, strategy and commercialization arm of Kentucky Space. The 27-year-old Twyman knew when he accepted the job that he would have his work cut out for him.

As president and CEO, the pressure was on Twyman to raise the capital that would enable Space Tango to accomplish its goal of partnering with space science programs, NASA and companies interested in novel, high-risk/high-value space technologies. To do so, Twyman knew he had to decide what Space Tango should focus on so that he could craft the right message to take to investors. With the end-of-year deadline looming, Twyman explained his challenge:

> Since I got the CEO job, my biggest challenge is making sure we focus on the right things and get the right message out. Obviously, the end goal is the money, but the right message is a subset of that. It's good that I come from the technical side because I can answer all the technical questions, but I explain everything like an engineer rather than from the customer's perspective. My big worry is learning how to pitch Space Tango fast enough so that we don't get passed up. I think we've got a really good idea, and I don't want to be saying in a few months, "Damn it, we messed up."

On a personal level, Twyman was motivated to make Space Tango a success. He had experienced more than his share of health problems growing up, and he believed that Space Tango's space mission could, among other things, help advance medical discoveries on Earth. As he explained:

> I spent a lot of time in hospitals when I was growing up. I was diagnosed with Type I diabetes when I was 16, then I had a bout with cancer right after I finished college. I did the whole chemo thing – lost my hair. The chemo room is a battlefield. I saw people die across the room from me. A good friend I grew up with died of cancer when he was 18 and you see that just wipe everybody out. The real motivation is the sorrow you see people go through in those hospitals. After watching that at a human level, you ask yourself if there is some way you can make a difference. At the moral level, we at Space Tango hope to contribute to fixing some of those medical challenges by looking at them in a different way. For the most part, the experiments in space have been focused on the astronauts' health – the six people in space rather than the 7 billion people on Earth.

Appendix 2: IMD Case Space Tango (B)

                                   - 2 -   IMD-7-1629

Kentucky's Best-kept Secret – Aerospace

When most people thought of Kentucky, they thought of bourbon and horses. But who would have thought that Kentucky could become a leader in the aerospace industry. That is exactly what Kris Kimel, president of Space Tango's parent company, Kentucky Science and Technology Corporation (KSTC), had set out to achieve (*refer to Exhibit 1 for an overview of KSTC's organization*).[1]

Based in Lexington, Kentucky, KSTC was established in 1987 as a private, non-profit corporation to develop innovation-driven, talent, research and development, and entrepreneurial companies in Kentucky. When technological advances that allowed miniaturization began revolutionizing consumer electronics and the world began to see ever-smaller laptop computers and cellphones, Kris recognized that spacecraft would also be affected. With NASA outsourcing much of its work to private industry, he thought, "Why can't miniature spacecraft and related space technology be designed and built in Kentucky?"

As a result, in 2005, KSTC, together with Morehead State University and the University of Kentucky and others, set up a lab in California's Silicon Valley. They collaborated with NASA engineers and Stanford University to learn about small satellite technology, including CubeSats – 10-centimeter cubes that were powered by solar panels and full of off-the-shelf technology.

CubeSats were invented in 1999 as an educational tool, and the number of deployments had increased since their first launch in 2003.[2] The cost of building and launching a CubeSat was about US$100,000, a small fraction of the cost of building and launching a big conventional satellite that could have a price tag of $50 million to $100 million. Their small size and weight (about one kilogram) made it easy for rockets to accommodate them. Thanks to cheap parts and the start of NASA's CubeSat Launch Initiative in 2010, which provided free rides to space, the format took off.

The proliferation of CubeSats orbiting Earth meant that these tiny boxes were transmitting terabytes of data that could be transformed into extremely useful and valuable information. They could monitor the production of bacterial proteins in space or provide clues about the economic health of countries, industries and individual businesses.

Taking a Giant Leap for Mankind

In 2006, KSTC established Kentucky Space (KS), an independent, non-profit enterprise comprised of space industry professionals who worked with university students and companies to design and build satellites and related technology. By 2010, KS had built and installed aluminum cubes called CubeLabs on the International Space Station (ISS)

The CubeLab research platform, which was born out of a need for repeatable/affordable research on the ISS, was a standardized platform for microgravity research experiments. KS built the first platform for another company, but then built on this work based on the belief that research in outer space could open the door to a deeper understanding of disease processes and

---

[1] Kris Kimel is also the chairman of Space Tango.

[2] CubeSats were invented by Bob Twiggs of Stanford University and Jordi Puig-Suri of California Polytechnic State University. Bob Twiggs has since moved to Morehead State University in Kentucky.

solutions because cells, molecules, genes, microbes, and the like behaved differently when there was no gravity. Microgravity experiments could also facilitate research on the development of drugs to treat various diseases. The goal was to identify insights that could be applied to research on Earth, which in turn could lead to faster time-to-market for new drug products, treatments or procedures.

Several early biomedical experiments had already been flown to the ISS, including an investigation into the microgravity effects on glioblastoma cancer cells by scientists hoping to gather knowledge for a deeper investigation into the effects of microgravity on this deadly form of cancer. According to Daniel Erb, a former KS engineer:

> If one change makes it more aggressive, maybe a similar change makes it less aggressive and then with that we can design better drugs that can target those specific areas in the cancer cell.[3]

In May 2011, KS launched the Exomedicine Institute (EMI) as a non-profit to study medical solutions in the microgravity environment of space.[4] It presented opportunities for potentially game-changing discoveries that could be applied on Earth. As Kris explained:

> Once you leave the Earth's gravitational pull, all assumptions about chemistry, disease behavior and cellular biology go out the window. Our hope is that these experiments will shed light in areas such as diabetes, cardiology, Alzheimer's and tissue regeneration.

Back Down on Earth

By 2013, aerospace products and parts had become Kentucky's largest export, accounting for $5.6 billion – 22% of the value of all Kentucky exports and more than any other product. According to Kris:

> We're clearly one of the global leaders in trying to work on and design this next generation of spacecraft and technology. Our specialty is building small high-value machines quickly and reliably. Some of the more cutting-edge aerospace technology is being developed in our state.

By March 2014, Kentucky Space and its partners had successfully launched three experimental nanosatellites (small satellites under 10 kilograms), from the US and Russia, including the KySat–2 on a Minotaur I rocket out of Wallops Island, Virginia on November 19, 2013 (*refer to Exhibit 2*). The satellites were orbiting about 600 kilometers above the Earth at 8 kilometers per second and sending data to ground stations in Kentucky (*refer to Exhibit 3*).

In 2014, KS planned to fly a regenerative medicine investigation involving planarian flatworms to the ISS in partnership with Tufts University in Boston, Massachusetts. Flatworms can regenerate themselves when cut anywhere along their length. Scientists were interested in exploring how the mechanism for regeneration would be affected by the microgravity/high-radiation environment of low-Earth orbit.

---

[3] "Kentucky Space Sends Experiment into Space." *Lex18.com*, May 16, 2011. <www.lex18.com/news/kentucky-space-sends-experiment-into-space> (accessed November 25, 2014).

[4] "At the ISS's orbital altitude, the gravity from the Earth is 88% of that at sea level. While the constant free fall of the ISS offers a perceived sensation of weightlessness, the environment on-board is not one of weightlessness or zero-gravity, instead it is often described as microgravity." (Source: Exomedicine Institute, www.exomedicine.com/index.php/faq).

The Launch of Space Tango

Established in July 2014 as the for-profit, marketing, strategy and commercialization arm of KS, Space Tango was focused on the entrepreneurial space marketplace, which included the design and development of entrepreneurial space solutions. Its capabilities included CubeSats, PocketQubes (*refer to Exhibit 4*) and other microsatellites and subsystems, satellite ground operations, spacecraft design and testing, and the development of novel technologies and experiments for the ISS. Space Tango collaborated with a number of companies, universities and organizations, which gave it access to the combined resources and capabilities of its partners including technical expertise and physical facilities (*refer to Exhibit 5*).

FedEx® Collaboration

In May 2014, an announcement was made about the launch of FedEx® Space Solutions and the FedEx Space Desk that would serve as a centralized logistics hub to move payloads safely between laboratories and launch sites. These new offerings were the culmination of two-and-a-half years of work by FedEx, during which time Space Tango provided consulting services to FedEx helping them to validate the market and figure out how to provide solutions to this new segment. The commercial space industry represented a growth opportunity for FedEx, since both small businesses and international players were increasingly entering the industry.

While there were many horror stories of irreplaceable payloads being ruined, the catalyst that led to Space Tango's collaboration with FedEx was an experiment that flew into orbit on STS-131 and returned on the following mission STS-132.[5] Once back on Earth, the payload was exposed to radiation, rendering the results void. Prior to the FedEx collaboration, there had been no real safe and/or reliable way to move space objects terrestrially. Space Tango and many others had been hand carrying CubeSats and other space assets to various locations to make sure they arrived safely and on time. However, this was logistically complicated for a number of reasons. Satellites, when packed in their shipping containers, resembled bombs, which often resulted in delays. Also commercial flights were often delayed or canceled. If the shipment did not make it to the launch site on time, Space Tango had to start a potential yearlong process all over again. On the return journey, payloads, especially biosensitive ones, needed to get back to the labs as soon as possible.

Space Tango trained employees on FedEx's Space Desk to understand the specific needs of the space industry so they could provide reliable terrestrial transport of clients' celestial packages, everything from satellites and related subsystems to biomedical materials bound for testing or use in space. It also helped produce a space-related training manual for FedEx.

The FedEx Space Desk allowed Space Tango to focus on design rather than worrying about moving its space assets on Earth. When the payloads returned, Space Tango had the peace of mind of knowing that FedEx knew the unique conditions in which things needed to be shipped and that when a payload came back, it came in a condition that was usable.

---

[5] The STS-131 was a multipurpose logistics module that was filled with science racks that were transferred to laboratories on the International Space Station (Source: NASA, www.nasa.gov/mission_pages/shuttle/shuttlemissions/sts131/main/index.html).

FedEx realized that many supply chain challenges could be solved with the help of information. In the aerospace industry, security, shipment integrity and supply chain efficiency were imperative to success. To meet the supply chain demands of the aerospace industry, FedEx used its sensor-based logistics offering – SenseAware.ₘ powered by FedEx (www.youtube.com/watch?v=ND3F4Y7MVkI) – to detect environmental variables such as temperature, light exposure, humidity, barometric pressure and location. Through wireless communication, it could transmit this data in near real-time to provide a continual, accurate picture of what was happening inside a shipment. This was particularly important for biomedical research which was often sensitive to environmental conditions and extremely difficult – if not impossible – to replace.

NASA's Space Act Agreement

In 2014, NASA approved a five-year extension of its Space Act agreement with KS for conducting research aboard the ISS National Laboratory.[6] Through NASA's Space Act Agreement, Space Tango could provide service to customers interested in taking advantage of its facilities aboard the ISS. Although it did not control the queue, Space Tango could influence it. With seven launches expected in the next two years, Space Tango was in a strong position to predict availability on the upcoming missions, so it had started selling slots for these flights.[7]

The Space Act agreement with NASA, together with the FedEx collaboration, helped to legitimize Space Tango's position in the space industry by giving it the visibility and credibility it needed to attract the brightest and best talent to Kentucky.

Twyman's Challenge: The Countdown is On

As a child growing up on a farm in Bardstown – in the heart of Kentucky bourbon country – Twyman never dreamed that he would have the opportunity to work in the aerospace industry, never mind as the CEO of an aerospace start-up in Kentucky. Before becoming CEO, Twyman, who graduated from the University of Kentucky with a BS and MS in Mechanical Engineering, had worked as an engineer at Kentucky Space for four years. When asked how he thought space research could impact everyday life on Earth, Twyman explained how it had affected him personally:

---

6 In accordance with the NASA Authorization Act of 2005, NASA operated a share of its US accommodations on the ISS as a national laboratory. In preparation for it to move from a construction phase to a utilization phase, it offered domestic entities (other than the US federal government) the opportunity to use the ISS. In 2011, KS signed a Space Act agreement with NASA to enable opportunities for space-based research, whereby KS served as the implementation partner for various commercial and university researchers. In turn, NASA provided on-orbit resources and limited launch and return opportunities.

7 The Crimean crisis that started in 2014, and the sanctions that soon followed, had caused some concern for Space Tango and others in the industry because it put the spotlight on the vulnerability of US space exploration. Since NASA's space shuttles were discontinued in 2011, there were no alternatives other than the Russian Soyuz capsule for transporting astronauts to the ISS. However, in September 2014, NASA announced that SpaceX and Boeing had been contracted to take astronauts to the ISS. With a goal of 2017 for the first crewed launch, the deal would end NASA's reliance on the Russians for transporting astronauts to the space station.

My immediate answer comes from a device that literally hasn't left my side in more than a decade. The core technology of the insulin pump I use to regulate my glucose levels as a Type I diabetic was initially developed for the Viking landers that were sent to Mars in the late 1970s. I can actually say the effect of our space economy is in my blood.

Twyman's most pressing challenge was to raise $1 million in equity by selling a 20% stake in Space Tango to investors – 40% non-dilutive and 60% dilutive.[8] Space Tango's initial sole investor was its parent company, KSTC.

With just five contract employees (two embedded systems engineers, a biomedical engineer and a salesperson) in addition to Twyman, Space Tango was able to generate some small sources of revenue from its consulting activities and patents. It also planned to generate revenue by leasing space on its TangoLab facility, which was due to be installed on the ISS in the summer of 2015. The novel TangoLab platform would give Space Tango's customers access to microgravity research. But Space Tango still needed additional capital to take it to the next level. Twyman's plan was to formulate Space Tango's strategy and develop a compelling message that he could use to sell it to potential investors by the end of 2014.

Space Tango targeted customers in the non-profit, academic, government and commercial sectors, including pharmaceutical, materials, biotechnology, agricultural biotechnology and personalized medicine companies. By offering its customers launch/transportation services, Space Tango could conduct regular research missions to the ISS. Its logistics, scientific, engineering and technical expertise allowed it to provide comprehensive support for payloads on flights to the ISS. It could tailor experiment design, payload design and integration services based on the needs of the investigation. Also, its operations center on the ground provided direct communication with astronauts to facilitate human-tended experiments and problem mitigation. And, working with FedEx, it could handle the terrestrial logistics of its clients' payloads.

Although it had several US competitors, Space Tango was more efficient and had a reputation for high integrity, speed and reliability, which were big selling points in the industry. There were no major international competitors, but that could change quickly. However, the barriers to entry were high and Space Tango had been quietly amassing the resources and capabilities to send missions to the ISS, but it needed to continue to move at a fast pace and raise capital or it risked losing its first-mover advantage.

While many considered Space Tango's location in Kentucky a disadvantage, Twyman believed it was a plus for a variety of reasons. It was less expensive to do business in Lexington than, say, Silicon Valley. The location helped Space Tango stay under the radar, which was important particularly for medical initiatives. Space Tango's access to Morehead State University's 21-meter dish high up in the mountains of Kentucky was also a distinct advantage because compared to those in big urban centers, the dish received strong signals due to the lack of interference or noise from other signal sources (*refer to Exhibit 6*). Furthermore, NASA was a very distributed organization, so no matter where Space Tango was located, traveling to one of NASA's locations would still be required.

---

[8] Dilutive equity dilutes the ownership percentage of current shareholders.

From Twyman's perspective, Space Tango had a services side and a product side. The services side included Space Tango's consulting services to FedEx on FedEx Space Solutions, as well as selling capability on its antenna and environmental testing systems. The capability part was not a long-term growth strategy, but it brought cash in the door. But as Twyman said, "The balancing act is when does it become a distraction."

The product side was focused on the TangoLab facility that would be installed on the ISS in 2015. The TangoLab platform would generate several sources of revenue. The second generation of the Lab product line would be a more biomedical-specific version. Space Tango planned to have this installed on the ISS in about 12 to 24 months. The vast majority of the $1 million in capital that Space Tango hoped to raise would be used for this project.

There were also some small opportunities in education and research. The highest-risk, highest-return opportunity was the Exomedicine Institute, which to date had mostly been self-funded because outside sources of funding had been sporadic and small. However, once the second Lab was installed on the ISS, Space Tango hoped that the EMI could achieve its objective of working with partners to identify opportunities where exomedicine experiments might help in the fight to improve the outcome of certain diseases. According to Twyman:

> If you discover something that can ameliorate a disease, that's huge. But while this is very true, it is also something I've seen many space companies bet all their marbles on. While we are hoping for success in this area, we aren't betting the works on it.

Twyman needed to finalize Space Tango's business model, homing in on those activities that had the best chance of moving the company forward, while managing the diverging objectives of its non-profit parent KS (which owned 51% of Space Tango) vs. the for-profit objectives of Space Tango. To kick-start the process, Twyman was planning to use the "Business Model Canvas" (*refer to Exhibit 7*). Sitting in his lab after a long day at the IdeaFestival,[9] he flicked on his computer and brought up an empty canvas. It was time to start filling in the blanks.

---

[9] The IdeaFestival is a week-long event sponsored in part by KSTC. It brings together 15,000 of the world's most forward thinkers, including entrepreneurs, business leaders, lifescience and healthcare innovators, educators, etc.

- 8 -   IMD-7-1629

Exhibit 1
Organization

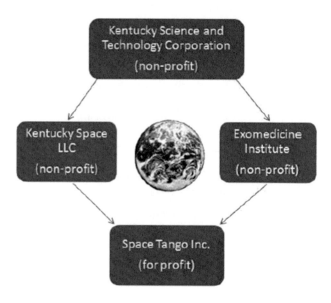

Source: Company information

Exhibit 2
Launch of KySat-2 on a Minotaur I Rocket on November 19, 2013
out of Wallops Island, Virginia

Source: Company information

Exhibit 3
Twyman Clements and Kris Kimel Tracking a Space Satellite
from Space Tango's Control Room

Source: Photo by Tom Eblen, *Lexington Herald-Leader*. <www.kentucky.com/2014/07/26
/3353120/tom-eblen-msus-space-center-proves.html#storylink=cpy> (accessed October 8, 2014).

Exhibit 4
CubeSat and PocketQube

CubeSat
The Engineering and Flight Models of KySat-2 in the Clean Room before Launch

The KySat–2 before Launch

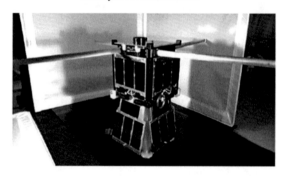

PocketQube

Source: Company information

IMD-7-1629

- 11 -

Exhibit 5
Space Tango's Lab

Source: Company information

Exhibit 6
21-Meter Radio Dish Space Tango Used for Satellite Communications
and Radio Astronomy

Source: Company information

IMD-7-1629

- 13 -

Exhibit 7
Business Model Canvas

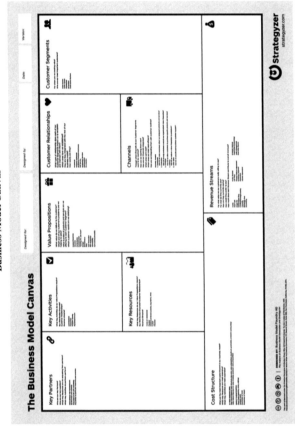

Source: Osterwalder, Alexander, Yves Pigneur and Tim Clark. *Business Model Generation: A Handbook for Visionaries, Game Changers, and Challengers*. Hoboken, NJ: Wiley, 2010. <www.businessmodelgeneration. com/canvas/bmc> (accessed November 25, 2014). This work is licensed under the Creative Commons Attribution-Share Alike 3.0 Unported License – http://creativecommons.org/licenses/by-sa/3.0/.

- 14 -   IMD-7-1629

Public Sources

The information in this case is based on interviews with Kentucky Science and Technology Corporation, Kentucky Space and Space Tango executives, company websites and the following public sources:

Boyd, Terry. "Why not Kentucky? Econ-dev Execs Kris Kimel, Ted Smith Agree We Could Be Space Research Center." *Insider Louisville*, April 19, 2013. <http://insiderlouisville.com/business/space/> (accessed November 25, 2014).

"CASIS Reaches Agreement with Kentucky Space to Advance Regenerative Research." CASIS Press Release, October 3, 2013. <www.iss- casis.org/NewsEvents/PressReleases/tabid/111/ArticleID/89/ ArtMID/586/CASIS-Reaches-Agreement-with-Kentucky-Space-to-Advance-Regenerative-Research.aspx> (accessed November 25, 2014).

Clements, Twyman. "Kentucky Has Seat at Space Exploration Table." *The Courier-Journal*, March 21, 2014. <www.courier-journal.com/story/opinion/2014/03/21/kentucky-seat-space-exploration-table/6708613/> (accessed November 25, 2014).

Eblen, Tom. "Morehead Space Program Shows Eastern Kentucky Can Aim High." *The Bluegrass and Beyond: Lexington-Leader Columnist Tom Eblen*, July 26, 2014. <tomeblen.bloginky.com/tag/space-tango/> (accessed November 25, 2014).

Eblen, Tom. "MSU's Space Center Proves Eastern Kentucky Can Aim High in Job Creation." *kentucky.com*, July 26, 2014. <www.kentucky.com/2014/07/26/3353120 tom-eblen-msus-space-center-proves.html?rh=1> (accessed November 25, 2014).

"FedEx Launches FedEx® Space Desk, A Centralized Logistics and Information Hub for Space Industry." *FedEx Newsroom*, May 19, 2004. <http://news.van.fedex.com/fedex-launches-fedex%C2%AE-space-desk-centralized-logistics-and-information-hub-space-industry > (accessed November 25, 2014).

Hill, Kevin. "Exploring the Final Frontier with FedEx® Space Solutions." *FedEx Blog*, May 20, 2014. <http://blog.van.fedex.com/fedex-space-solutions> (accessed November 25, 2015).

Jones, Nicola. "Mini Satellites Prove Their Scientific Power: Proliferation of 'CubeSats' Offers Fresh and Fast Way to Gather Space Data." *Nature*, April 16, 2014. <www.nature.com/news/mini-satellites-prove-their-scientific-power-1.15051> (accessed November 25, 2014).

"Kentucky Space Sends Experiment into Space." *Lex18.com*, May 16, 2011. <www.lex18.com/news/kentucky-space-sends-experiment-into-space> (accessed November 25, 2014).

"LEADER Q&A – A Conversation with Mandy Lambert." *Janus Institute*, June 27, 2014. <http://www.senseaware.com/who-benefits/aerospace/> (accessed November 25, 2014).

"Nonreimbursable Space Act Agreement between the National Aeronautics and Space Administration, Lyndon B. Johnson Space Center and Kentucky Space, LLC, for New Operation of a Multilab Aboard the International Space Station National Laboratory." *NASA*, July 8, 2014. <www.nasa.gov/sites/default/files/files/Kentucky_SAA_17635_7-8-2014_signed.pdf> (accessed November 25, 2014).

Samuels, David. "Inside a Startup's Plan to Turn a Swarm of DIY Satellites into an All-Seeing Eye." *Wired*, June 18, 2013. <www.wired.com/2013/06/startup-skybox/> (accessed November 25, 2014).

Stromberg, Joseph. "Russia Is Kicking NASA out of the International Space Station in 2020." *Vox*, May 13, 2014. <www.vox.com/2014/5/13/5714650/russia-just-evicted-nasa-from-the-international-space-station> (November 25, 2015).

IMD-7-1630
19.01.2015

SPACE TANGO: DANCING WITH THE STARS (B)

Researcher Beverley Lennox prepared this case under the supervision of Professor Carlos Cordón as a basis for class discussion rather than to illustrate either effective or ineffective handling of a business situation.

As Twyman looked at the blank Business Model Canvas on his screen, the following thought was running through his mind:

> I need to get this together and hit the road and raise some $$$.

As he began filling in the blanks, he reflected on the feedback he had received that day from the local entrepreneurs who had participated in the weeklong IdeaFestival.

The next morning, Twyman was in his office for an hour before heading back to the IdeaFestival. He made some final tweaks to the Business Model Canvas (*refer to Exhibit 1*) and then sent it to Kris Kimel, the chairman of Space Tango, for his feedback.

Next, he started to work on a draft of his "elevator pitch." Twyman wanted to make sure he got it right. He knew he had to simplify it, and as he was working through it, a familiar thought came back him:

> I think we've got a really good idea, and I don't want to be saying in a few months, "Damn it, we messed up."

IMD-7-1630

-2-

Exhibit 1
Space Tango's Business Model Canvas

References

Alsever, Jennifer. 2015. Startups . . . inside giant companies. Fortune. April 26. http://fortune.com/2015/04/26/startups-inside-giant-companies/. Accessed August 20, 2015.

Cordón, Carlos, and Beverley Lennox. 2015. Space Tango: Dancing with the stars (A). IMD case study no. IMD-7-1629. January.

Ebhardt, Tommaso. 2014. Ferrari to boost production to keep pace with super rich. September 11. BloombergBusiness. http://www.bloomberg.com/news/articles/2014-09-11/ferrari-to-boost-production-to-keep-pace-with-super-rich. Accessed August 20, 2015.

Foy, Henry. 2014. Ferrari profits soar despite reducing car production numbers. February 18. Financial Times. http://www.ft.com/intl/cms/s/0/48c59732-9891-11e3-a32f-00144feab7de.html#axzz3bXCCqeFV. Accessed August 20, 2015.

Johnson, Mark W., Clayton M. Christensen, Henning Kagermann. 2008. Reinventing your business model. Harvard Business Review. December. https://hbr.org/2008/12/reinventing-your-business-model. Accessed August 20, 2015.

Marx, Willem. 2015. How does Uber make money? BloombergBusiness. May 30. http://www.bloomberg.com/news/videos/b/48bcbc81-c457-4c71-809c-823da150b5a3. Accessed August 20, 2015.

Osterwalder, Alexander. 2004. The business model ontology: A proposition in a design science approach. Thesis. Université de Lausanne, Ecole des Hautes Etudes Commerciales. http://www.hec.unil.ch/aosterwa/PhD/Osterwalder_PhD_BM_Ontology.pdf. Accessed August 20, 2015.

Osterwalder, Alexander. 2011. The story of a bestselling management book. Available on Slideshare, Slide 49. http://www.slideshare.net/Alex.Osterwalder/bmgen-the-story-of-a-bestselling-management-book. Accessed August 20, 2015.

Osterwalder, Alexander and Yves Pigneur. 2010. Business Model Generation. A Handbook for Visionaries, Game Changers, and Challengers. John Wiley & Sons.

Schmidt, Eric, and Jonathan Rosenberg with Alan Eagle. 2014. How Google Works. John Murray (Kindle e-book version).

Sinek, Simon. 2009. Start with WHY. Portfolio and Penguin. See also Simon Sinek's TED Talk, How great leaders inspire action, September 2009. https://www.ted.com/talks/simon_sinek_how_great_leaders_inspire_action

Strategyzer. N.d. Business model canvas. This work is licensed under the Creative Commons Attribution-Share Alike 3.0 Unported License. http://www.businessmodelgeneration.com/canvas/bmc

Tzuo, Tien. 2015. Why this CEO believes an MBA is worthless. Fortune. April 27. http://fortune.com/2015/04/27/tien-tzuo-starting-your-own-business/. Accessed August 20, 2015.

Weinberger, Matt. 2015. Why Coca-Cola wants to fund the next billion-dollar startup. *Business Insider*. May 14. http://www.businessinsider.com/coca-cola-is-in-the-business-of-bottling-billion-dollar-startups-2015-5. Accessed August 20, 2015.

Conclusions

The aim of this book has been to provide executives with an understanding of how big data is substantially transforming "traditional" businesses, that is, those created before the big data tsunami. We have used examples of companies from different industries, such as toy company LEGO and Dutch healthcare company Mediq, to describe how they used big data to transmute their companies' respective DNAs.

Our objective has also been to provide an executive guide on how to embark on the big data journey. The process we propose is based on the findings of our research in terms of how companies have successfully created value using big data. It is a process that uses novel methods, most of them developed over the last 5 years. While they have proved to be the best so far to obtain good results, they are still fresh and being improved.

© Springer International Publishing Switzerland 2016

137

C. Cordon et al., *Strategy is Digital*, Management for Professionals,
DOI 10.1007/978-3-319-31132-6_7

7.1   The Big Impact of Big Data

The big data tsunami has reached a tipping point. The smartphone phenomenon in particular has dramatically changed society in the last few years to the extent that a majority of consumers and executives use and need their smartphones at all times and would be lost without them.

It is clear that CEOs are aware of the big data impact. For almost 20 years it was common in executive meetings for participants to have their laptops open in front of them. Today they are mostly using smartphones, tablets, phablets, wearables and other devices. This has impacted the views of the C-suite to such an extent that according to The Conference Board CEO Challenge® survey the number one hot topic for CEOs in 2013 and 2014 was big data.

Traditional companies like GE or BBVA are making big data their top strategic priority. Both companies—traditional industrial and banking conglomerates respectively—are redefining their mission to become leaders in their particular fields in this new digital world, and they are taking fundamental strategic decisions in that direction.

GE is focusing on big data analytics. Its CEO stated in his 2015 letter to shareholders that the company's mission is "to invent the next industrial era" by leading "the merger of machines and analytics through the Industrial Internet to drive new levels of productivity" (GE 2015). Accordingly, it started divesting more than $200 billion worth of businesses that were not related to its digital future in order to focus on the industrial internet business.

BBVA, one of the top banks in the world, replaced its president in 2015 with the head of its digital banking, demonstrating the bank's commitment to its digital transformational plans. Further, "the bank said that it was closing its digital banking unit, signaling that digital innovation will be a priority across BBVA's management structure" (Neumann 2015).

Throughout this book we have argued that most companies should be following the example of such leaders and undertaking their own digital journey.

7.2   All Companies Are Affected

It is not possible to assess which companies or industries will be most affected because nobody can predict when one or several companies will disrupt their ecosystem. We have pointed several times to the example of Uber, which has dramatically changed the ecosystem of traditional taxi companies and drivers. No one could have predicted that.

A recent study by the Global Center for Digital Business Transformation, An IMD and Cisco Initiative, ranked a number of industries based on how much big data would disrupt them according to executives in their industries (see Fig. 7.1). Pharmaceuticals was last on the list, indicating that executives in pharmaceutical companies felt that their business was least at risk of disruption (Bradley et al. 2015).

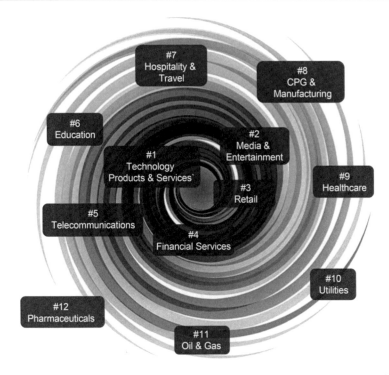

Fig. 7.1 Digital disruption by industry (*Source*: Global Center for Digital Business Transformation, an IMD and Cisco Initiative, 2015)

This is especially interesting because throughout this book, we have used the example of Mediq—a key player in the pharmaceuticals ecosystem—to highlight how it has fundamentally disrupted its ecosystem. The inference is that executives have a deep knowledge of their industries and companies based on past patterns. However, the future shaped by big data is very different and most executives have little experience of such monumental change and how to evaluate its consequences.

7.3   The Challenge Is to Adapt to a Revolution

Big data is considered to be a revolution in that it means asking new relevant questions rather than trying to answer old ones. In general, companies that have invested in big data but are still trying to answer old questions have found the results disappointing. Those that formulated new questions have spawned new business models with great results.

Mediq executives pushed themselves to ask new questions such as, "How do we take better care of the patient?" and "How do we reduce the number of hospitalizations due to incorrect use of medication?" They modified the ecosystem to such an extent that instead of just moving boxes around they now advise doctors on the best medications to prescribe and follow up with patients who appear not to be respecting their recommended treatments. They are surprised that no pharmaceutical company has approached them to collaborate on prescription management despite the fact that if Mediq were to be informed about better drugs than those currently being prescribed, this could lead to changes in the medication of tens of thousands of patients in less than a month.

One well-known pharmaceutical giant invested heavily in providing its sales force with iPads to improve the way sales representatives exchanged information with medical practitioners, but so far the results have proved meagre. They call it digitization. The problem is that the company is using big data to help its sales force answer old questions about visits to medical doctors, which drugs to promote, sales evolution and so on.

Changing that ecosystem would mean changing the role played by the pharmaceutical company, as Mediq did. In the new ecosystem, the pharmaceutical company may no longer need a sales force because pharmacy companies could play that role using big data. Such a change would of course be brutal and revolutionary since the sales force constitutes the majority of employees in many pharmaceutical companies.

Adapting to the big data tsunami might signify a revolution for some companies, but others may only need to make adjustments. The degree of adaptation will depend on the extent to which the company's role in the ecosystem is going to change, on the changes started by other players and on the company's ambition to go beyond its existing limits.

Organizations such as GE and BBVA are conglomerates made up of many different businesses so you would expect that some businesses would be more radically affected than others and therefore the level of change will not be the same across all of them. In such cases the revolution is so big that the corporation would need to focus on the businesses that can be most dramatically improved by using big data.

Still, this kind of change is very different and new, and corporations have a difficult time embarking on such a journey. One corporation with more than $5 billion in sales and more than ten different business units is going through a somewhat surprising journey. The CEO pushed the business unit heads to launch big data initiatives to learn and see how they might improve their businesses. None of them tried to do so, arguing that they were too busy running the existing business, that they were expected to deliver results and that, anyway, they did not even know how to start such an initiative. Thus, no action was taken at the top level to develop big data. However, unbeknown to the top management and the CEO, a manager in one of the business units, who had been allocated a budget to replace some of the IT equipment that was becoming obsolete, invested in big data and furtively started the journey in that business unit. Eventually, of course, the CEO and the rest of the top management learned about the initiative and the corporation is following up on it.

In our opinion it is not that the business unit heads were resistant to change. Rather, they simply did not understand this new paradigm. It is hard to lead something totally unknown.

7.4 The Technology Behind Big Data Is Constantly Evolving

The lack of understanding about the technology behind big data is due to the fact that it is constantly evolving. For this reason we have avoided describing any specific technology in this book. Figure 7.2 illustrates the technology landscape in 2015 (Cisco 2015). It is fragmented and requires specialist technical knowledge to understand it.

The problem of deciding which technologies to use to collect and use big data remains unresolved and can be expanded to include information technology providers in general. The dilemma is between integration vs. best of breed.

Some software companies base their offer on the possibility of integrating the existing IT systems and software with new developments. This, they argue, makes it easy to exchange information and integrate new ways of working with the existing infrastructure.

Other companies argue that it is better to choose the best systems and software for the current tasks, and then develop integration systems to create a real-time exchange layer between best-of-breed systems. The argument here is that the analysis that needs to be made is so specific that no general tool can do it effectively.

This is thus a management dilemma for which there is no ready-made solution. Executives will have to manage the fact that the objectives of integration and specialization are both legitimate but none of the technology available at this stage can totally fulfill their respective needs. Similar to what we saw from a management perspective in the LEGO case in Chap. 2, executives need to navigate this dilemma by understanding the advantages and challenges of both options and accepting that the best decision is going to change over time.

We recommend shifting the focus from the technology details to managing the team, particularly as it will be made up of several types of specialists:

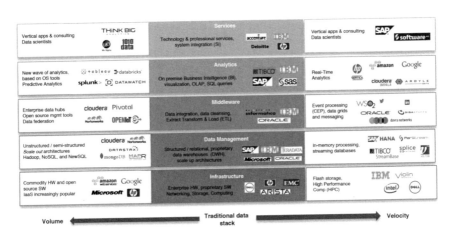

Fig. 7.2 The big data technology landscape in 2015 (Cisco 2015)

- Those specialized in analyzing data (the data scientists)
- Those specialized in data management infrastructure (the IT infrastructure specialists)
- Those specialized in finding the right questions to ask
- And perhaps those representing the other players in the ecosystem.

It is also important to be aware that specialists will have a natural bias toward technologies that they have worked with and know well. Logically, specialists prefer to work with methods and tools that they are familiar with and tend to be skeptical about big data tools that they do not know.

Given that technology is constantly evolving, willingness to experiment, learn and fail from time to time is crucial. This is why we recommend developing a portfolio of initiatives rather than just one. Some will succeed, others will fail. This is what companies that are succeeding in the big data journey are doing.

7.5   Adopting Big Data Requires Unlearning

On the big data journey, past experience can sometimes be a liability rather than an asset, so a lot of unlearning may be required. We illustrate this point with two examples from our research on big data in sports.

We interviewed two world-renowned coaches, one in triathlon and one in swimming, about the use of big data in sports. According to the swimming coach, "you can't win a gold Olympic medal without big data; gold medals are won by tenths of a second. That might just mean swimming with your shoulder in a position that is one millimeter higher." According to the triathlon coach, "The data we use comes from our eyes, and our ears (. . .). The only data analysis we do is in our head (. . .) (It) keeps mentally fragile athletes from worrying about data that is meaningless to their race-day performance, and can be a major disruption to their training." Clearly these two opinions are antithetical, yet both coaches are experts in their fields. It is even more striking considering that one of the triathlon disciplines is swimming.

We found a similar situation in many companies. It is not that some senior executives resist change and others do not. Rather, it is their experience—which is behind their successful careers—that defines their strong views about the value of data and the learning acquired throughout their careers.

This implies that executives need to "unlearn" by discarding past experiences and learning and, in particular, suspending judgment based on past experiences. They must also be willing to test new big data tools for long enough to understand their strengths.

One of the fundamental changes being ushered in by the big data tsunami is that experience could become almost irrelevant. A well-known example is Amazon, which replaced experts with big data.

> *When Amazon started out as a bookshop, it employed a team of experts to recommend new books to readers based on what they had already bought. As the company grew and accumulated data, it realized that using big data to automate recommendations based on millions of readers' preferences brought far more sales to the company than the experts' experience.*

Similarly, we have found that on the big data journey, often what was valuable experience in the past loses its value after the implementation of big data. Understandably, experts have a hard time accepting that the worthiness of the experience they have accumulated over many years, sometimes even decades, has been annihilated by big data.

The key is to be willing to experiment, to initiate a portfolio of initiatives and to learn. Young people are often believed to be better at implementing these technologies because they have nothing to lose and are willing to experiment and learn.

7.6 This Book Is a Roadmap to Big Data

No two big data journeys will be the same and not all strategies will imply that a company has to undergo the kind of transmutation that Mediq did. Organizations like Fedex may choose to make the core of their business digital and adapt their products and services to a digital ecosystem. Others may simply develop a strong digital strategy without changing their essence.

Leaders need to observe the ecosystem in which their company operates in order to understand how big data will impact them, and make a decision on the most appropriate strategy on that basis. This is not always straightforward. In Chap. 5 we explained how logistics companies were lagging when it came to adopting big data because although it may seem easy enough to implement, the reality is that too many players in an immense ecosystem need to agree and take concerted action, and that is not happening yet.

Executives are in a difficult position. They are seeking answers to "old" questions using big data and inevitably they are frustrated because the digital revolution implies formulating new questions, which is not easy. In many cases, it is so widely accepted that certain things cannot be changed that people do not even try to do so. Mediq had never before considered the possibility of issuing prescriptions as this was the prerogative of medical doctors. But by raising new out-of-the-box questions and designing a new business model founded on big data, the company was able to take on roles that it had previously not imagined possible.

To help open minds, it is worth exploring what others have done, visiting companies that are successfully completing the journey, and having conversations with executives who have already gone through the experience and exchanging know-how with them. Organizations that are successfully navigating the big data journey are those that were able to unlearn in order to see new possibilities and reinvent themselves.

In Chap. 6 we provided a framework to use as a roadmap (see Fig. 6.1). The first step is to clarify your company's purpose in the new digital landscape, its **WHY**. The second step is to prepare a **business model canvas** (or map) to present your company clearly and simply in a snapshot. The **profit formula** is then used to determine how the company will make money. Finally, for managing the business we propose applying the **Lean Startup** methodology, which is based on an ongoing cycle of testing, measuring results and implementing lessons learned, because in the big data era, things move fast and businesses need to be managed dynamically to survive.

7.7 A New Exciting World Ahead

The big data tsunami is fundamentally redefining the way people live and work and how companies function. The big data era has reached a tipping point in that there is now enough data and processing power to do many things that seemed like science-fiction just a few years ago, and the amount of data being collected is growing exponentially all the time, as are the technological capabilities to handle it.

This is opening up a whole new world of opportunities for organizations. It is also changing the way we understand business. Where once we defined business in terms of industries, strategic planning, making decisions under uncertainty and ensuring information was accurate, today we talk about it in terms of ecosystems, business models, formulating new questions and knowing what consumers want.

The big data journey is about discovering new things. A renowned business consultant recently claimed that everything that can be said about big data in value chains is, for the time being, speculative. We believe that this book demonstrates that big data is having a real impact on value chains. It is not just speculation. Several companies are already creating great business opportunities in the value chain using big data. We suggest that you follow in their footsteps to successfully embark on the big data revolution. Our aim with this book is to help you do just that, and we hope you succeed in this fascinating journey.

References

Bradley, Joseph, Jeff Loucks, James Macaulay, Andy Noronha, and Michael Wade. Digital Vortex—How digital disruption is redefining industries. IMD, Cisco, June 2015. http://www. imd.org/uupload/IMD.WebSite/DBT/Digital_Vortex_06182015.pdf. Accessed August 11, 2015.

GE. 2015. 2014 annual report. CEO letter. http://www.ge.com/ar2014/ceo-letter/. Accessed August 11, 2015.

Neumann, Jeanette. 2015. Spain's BBVA appoints new president. Wall Street Journal. May 4.

Valente, Marco, IMD VC2020 Forum Presentation, May 2015.